S.H.E.
WHO BELIEVED

Redefining life through God's Grace

S.H.E.
WHO BELIEVED

Redefining life through God's Grace

by :

REV. ANDREA D. LEWIS, Ph.D

VINE
PUBLISHING

Vine Publishing's name and logo are trademarks of Vine Publishing, Inc.

ISBN: 979-8-9867471-5-6 (paperback)
ISBN: 979-8-9867471-6-3 (e-book)

Library of Congress Cataloging-in-Publication Data
Library of Congress Control Number: 2022921071

Published by Vine Publishing, Inc.
New York, NY
www.vinepublish.com

Printed in the United States of America

Dedication

Rose Marie Dais Lewis – My Mother
Adeline Williams Dais – My Maternal Grandmother
Blanche Elizabeth Taylor Chase – My Paternal Grandmother
Louise Mallory Chandler – My Adopted Grandmother
Adrienne Patricia Lewis – My Sister
All of my Spelman College Daughters

Table of Contents

····················

Opening Prayer

....

How lovely is your dwelling place, O Lord of hosts! My soul longs, indeed it faints for the courts of the Lord; my heart and my flesh sing for joy to the living God. (Psalm 84:1-2 NRSV**)

Dear Most Merciful and Omnipresent God,

Thank you for bringing each of us to this space and place. We invite your sweet and ever-lasting Spirit to move freely amongst us. Dwell in each of our hearts. Equip us, challenge us, comfort us, teach us, and guide us into your way.
In Jesus' name.
Amen.

Introduction

....

To the beautiful woman reading this devotional memoir, it did not come into your hands by accident. God makes no mistakes. Even though my goal is to center this book on women, I love this quote by Albert Einstein: "Coincidence is God's way of remaining anonymous." Our encounter as author and reader is divinely orchestrated by God.

And as you turn these pages:

Read with the strength of Harriet Tubman, who was steadfast in her mission.

Read with the fortitude of Sojourner Truth, who reminded us, "Ain't I a woman?"

Read with the purpose of Michelle Obama, who led with grace and class.

Read with the persistence of Eleanor Roosevelt, who advocated for all.

Read with the independence of Fannie Lou Hamer, who was sick and tired of being sick and tired.

Read with the loyalty of Coretta Scott King and Betty Shabazz, for they remind us to stand by our men.

Read with the anticipated wealth of Oprah, because it's coming.

Read with the talents of Beyoncé, who always reminds us that "girls run the world".

Read with the sass of Maya Angelou, who reminds us that we are phenomenal.

Read with the power of your ancestors, whose spirits live inside of you.

Shortly after my childhood crush, Michael Jackson, passed away in 2009, a documentary chronicling the preparation for his last concert tour was released. My favorite scene in *This is It* shows Michael describing how he wants *The Way You Make Me Feel* to sound. He tells the band to play the chords in a particular manner and to linger on specific notes. He said, "You gotta let it simmer. You got a moment where it has to simmer. You're not letting it simmer. Just bathe in the moonlight. You have to let it simmer."

I started writing this book shortly before I got married in 2002. My then-neighbor asked me to facilitate a workshop at a women's retreat at her church. She said I reminded her of a virtuous woman, which was the theme of her church's event. As I created the content for my workshop, I thought it would be great to share my ideas in a book, for other women to read. As beautiful of an idea as I thought such a book would be, my plan was not God's plan. I kept the journal with my beginning notes and book outline, but it never materialized. Why? Because God had not yet finished letting me simmer. Like a good pot of chili or soup that is not mouthwatering and savory until it has sat on low heat for a while, God had not yet fully prepared me to minister to women. I had not gone through enough experiences to give a powerful and useful testimony. I had to wait until the hurt and pain had passed. I had to overcome and persevere. I had to find joy and success. I had to simmer.

This book's title, *S.H.E. Who Believed: Redefining Life Through God's Grace,* is grounded in Luke 1:45, which says, *"And blessed is She Who Believed that there would be a fulfillment of what was spoken to her by the Lord."* Often, I see clothing, bags, and trinkets with the saying, "She believed, so she did." I always felt that something was missing from that phrase. Something big is definitely missing. A woman cannot simply believe, then it automatically happens. I cannot believe I will be successful, and then success happens. Belief takes faith, prayer, preparation, time, and, sometimes, heartache and tears. Belief takes work and action. And, most importantly, as the scripture confirms, the action has to be ordained by God. I may want success, and I may even have a vision of what success looks like to me, but it is not successful until God ordains the desire. A woman cannot believe without the fulfillment of has been spoken to her by God. Whatever your fulfillment is, it happens in God's will and God's perfect timing.

S.H.E. Who Believed also centers on redefining yourself through God's grace. When I was a teenager, I participated in a three-year confirmation class at a Lutheran Church. I cannot tell you all that I learned, but one definition that forever remains in my heart and head is that of grace. The pastor taught us that grace is "God's love given freely." I imagine I should remember more from confirmation class, but that definition has seen me through many hard times. Grace is the backbone of God's love. And, God's grace is sufficient.

This devotional memoir is a faith-based journey of moving on after loss, accepting a new normal, and charting a new course with God's direction and grace. If you are going through a loss or change in your life, this book is for you. I hope that my mess, which became my message and my test, and, in turn, became my testimony, will help you out of the valley and up to the mountain top.

As you begin reading this book, don't forget that God's will and love are within you. God has already worked it out, but you have to be willing to let God use you. My prayer is that this book will minister to you and heal your spirit.

When you finish *S.H.E. Who Believed*, and after pondering the 15 steps to redefining your life, share it with another woman. You may also choose to use it in a group Bible study or for a women's ministry activity. However you choose to experience these pages, do it together—reflect together, redefine together, build together, and pray together.

INTRODUCTION DEVOTIONAL

How Has God Said Yes to You?

> *For in him every one of God's promises is a "Yes." For this reason it is through him that we say the "Amen," to the glory of God.* (2 Corinthians 1:20)

Before we delve into the upcoming chapters and focus on the concept of redefining, let's reflect on God's 'yes' moments in your life.

When the world may have told you no, how did God tell you yes?

1.

2.

3.

4.

5.

We often dwell in the roadblocks and closed doors in our lives, but we should always reflect on God's 'yes' moments. Those 'yes' moments bring us joy and remind us of God's promises You may not have five 'yes' experiences to write down in the blanks above, but as you read the coming pages, more 'yes' moments may come to your mind. I suspect that you will think of more than five in your life as you read and reflect. So I added five more opportunities for you to explore and write down.

Come back to this page and add them below when you are ready to record your thoughts.

6.

7.

8.

9.

10.

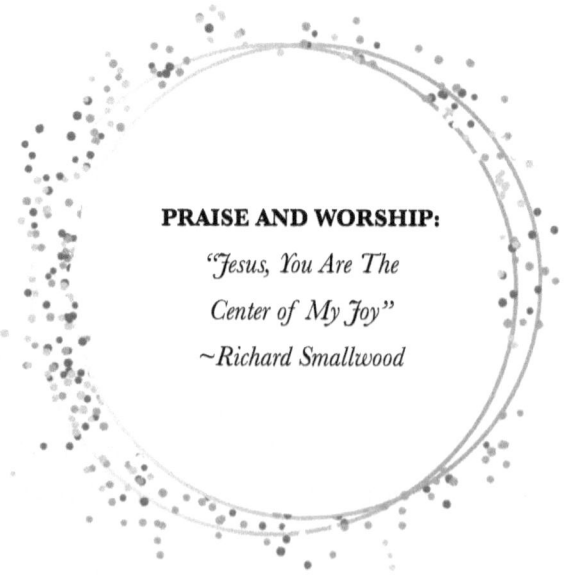

PRAISE AND WORSHIP:

"Jesus, You Are The
Center of My Joy"
~Richard Smallwood

Dear Gracious God,

When we get bogged down in negativity,
allow us to always recenter ourselves
in the 'yes' moments of our lives. The
'yes' moments allow us to see you, but
sometimes we forget that you are in the 'no'
moments as well. The 'yes' moments fill our
hearts with joy and show us your promises
in real life. Help us to remember that 'yes'
feeling in all that we say and do today. Be
with us and keep us in the center of our joy.
In your Son's name, we believe all things to
be true and we say together in one accord
with other readers.
Amen.

Chapter 1: A Time for Everything

For everything there is a season, and a time for every matter under heaven: a time to be born, and a time to die; a time to plant, and a time to pluck up what is planted; a time to kill, and a time to heal; a time to break down, and a time to build up; a time to weep, and a time to laugh; a time to mourn, and a time to dance; a time to throw away stones, and a time to gather stones together; a time to embrace, and a time to refrain from embracing; a time to seek, and a time to lose; a time to keep, and a time to throw away; a time to tear, and a time to sew; a time to keep silence, and a time to speak; a time to love, and a time to hate; a time for war, and a time for peace. (Ecclesiastes 3:1-8)

After I finished college and purchased a home, I was ready for the next step: marriage. In my waiting on God, I wrote a list of characteristics I desired in a husband. Not all of my requirements were religious, but they were my personal desires. About five years and many dates later, I thought I met him. He was my dad's mentee, who seemed to spend more time at my parents' house than I did. He was there for Sunday dinner and holidays. He was there in times of celebration and times of sadness. It therefore seemed a natural fit for us to start dating. Our first date was in March, we were engaged in September, and we married the following June.

While wedding planning, I experienced three warning signs but did not pay attention. First, my dad, who probably knew me best, told me not to marry this man. Although my fiancé was my dad's student and mentee, my dad was not in agreement with our marriage. I still remember our conversation, and I brushed his concerns off as insignificant and just him wanting me to stay "daddy's little girl." My dad's feelings were unbeknownst to my fiancé, especially since my dad had given his blessing to marry me.

The second warning came from a Sunday School student. My fiancé visited my church and attended my Sunday School class. After class, one of my first graders looked at me and said, "I do not like him." She was not sassy or rude, but spoke with the innocence of a child. I brushed her comment off as a child who was upset because I announced I would not be teaching Sunday School after my wedding.

The third warning, and the most spiritual, came from a stranger in Home Depot. My fiancé and I were shopping for renovation materials for a home we had recently purchased. A stranger stopped me in an aisle and quietly asked me if the gentleman I was with was my husband. I answered, "No, he is my fiancé." The man only said, "Do not marry him," and vanished to the next aisle as quietly as he had appeared next to me. I brushed this man off as crazy. What would this stranger know about my fiancé or me?

The spiritual aspect of the Home Depot encounter has stayed

with me. The man did not really walk up the aisle, nor did he walk back down the aisle. He appeared in front of me, engaged in brief conversation, then left as quickly as he came. As a detail-oriented person, I cannot tell you what he was wearing or anything else about him other than that he was a soft-spoken older Black man. I do remember there being something special about him. The man was real, but his presence had an aura. He was plain-clothed but majestic. I didn't realize it at the moment, but looking back on it, he was an angel. If you have never had an encounter with an angel, it is difficult to describe, and each person's experience is different.

Wedding planning and counseling continued with a few bumps, but nothing significant enough to halt our upcoming nuptials. The early years of our marriage were uneventful and spent like most newlyweds trying to co-exist in the same space. We made plans for the future, discussed children, finished a home renovation, and he completed a master's degree.

When it came time for family planning, our journey began with many complications. After no success with conceiving a baby, I went to see two gynecologists. They both said I would not be able to conceive naturally and would need the assistance of Clomid, which was a drug to stimulate my ovaries, or in vitro fertilization. We also explored the prospect of adoption and made an appointment with the local county adoption office.

On the morning of our adoption meeting, I also happened to have an appointment with yet another gynecologist, to get a third and final opinion regarding my fertility challenges. After providing the usual urine sample, I waited in an exam room. When this new doctor walked in, and she was looking at my paperwork, she asked why I was there specifically. I started to tell her about the previous doctors' recommendations for Clomid or in vitro fertilization, but then she suddenly interrupted me. "You are pregnant!", she exclaimed. I was in absolute disbelief. God had intervened! Our prayers had been answered!

My pregnancy was going well except for morning sickness, and all of our doctor appointments were without cause for concern. In my twenty-third week of pregnancy, I experienced the overwhelming need to push. Having never been pregnant before, I didn't realize the severity of the situation, especially since I still wasn't in pain.

As I drove myself to the doctor's office, I called my doctor, husband, and parents. When I arrived, they immediately took me to an exam room. Since it was lunchtime, many nurses and doctors were at lunch, unaware that I was waiting. With the continued feeling of having to push and now bleeding, I yelled out into the hall and a doctor finally came running. At this point, I wasn't having any pain, just the need to push. She determined that the baby was coming out, but there was not enough time to administer medicine to strengthen the baby's lungs. The hospital was next to the medical offices, so I was quickly wheeled through an underground tunnel to the hospital's Women's Center and into a delivery room. The neonatologist on duty shared all the concerns he had about resuscitating a premature baby at 23 weeks of gestation.

Again, all of this was happening so fast. We were in a daze, not understanding the complexities of the situation. Once I did feel pain, there was no time for an epidural, so I pushed and pushed until baby Micah was born. He was placed under a warming light in my room, for my husband and parents to see. I could not imagine the physical pain of birthing a larger baby, because delivering that almost two-pound baby was painful. I think the physical pain, coupled with the emotional pain, has been the worst of my life.

I spent the night in the hospital and then went home the next day, childless. With my milk coming in and the unreal events of the last 24 hours, my husband and I rode home in silence. I have always felt this was the beginning of the end of our marriage. Neither of us dealt well with the loss.

In the days and weeks after my baby's death, it was difficult to breathe. It was taxing just to put one foot in front of the other. I didn't know how I was going to press on through life. Have you ever been in this space and place? God seemed far away, even though I called on him daily. I did not think anyone in my immediate family understood my pain. My husband shut down, my mom tried but couldn't understand, and my dad just wanted me to stop crying.

After a series of follow-up doctor's appointments and MRIs, I was diagnosed with an incompetent cervix, which is a condition when weak cervical tissue causes or contributes to premature birth. Within three months, I was pregnant again and, at 12 weeks of gestation, at my doctor's recommendation, underwent a cervical cerclage, a procedure to stitch the cervix closed. I stayed on bed rest until my thirty-sixth week. I was scared and nervous, spending most of my time engaged in prayer and meditation.

At 34 weeks, my cerclage was removed and a healthy baby boy was born. Since his birth, Christian has been a wonderful source of joy and a living witness of God's immeasurable blessings. Life with baby Christian was a period of growth for me as a new mother experiencing many firsts in her child's development.

Two and a half years later, I became pregnant again. The news this time was bittersweet, as I learned on the same day as my pregnancy confirmation that my dad had cancer. Then came another cerclage and six months of bed rest, which was a little more challenging as I assisted my mom with my dad's care and chemotherapy treatments.

Baby Alexander came into this world as a healthy baby boy. His strong and caring personality has been present since birth. He is another living example of God's promises.

The doctors said I would not be able to conceive naturally. But I did just that, with God's help, in God's timing, and with God's blessing.

Ecclesiastes shares that there is a time for everything and a season for every activity under the heavens. It seemed that my marriage experienced all the seasons of the beginning verses of Ecclesiastes. It is a relationship I do not regret because, despite the differences my husband and I had, our greatest accomplishments and beautiful legacy are our three sons, Micah, Christian, and Alexander.

CHAPTER 1: DEVOTION

Praying Like Hannah

> *She made this vow: "O Lord of hosts, if only you will look on the misery of your servant, and remember me, and not forget your servant, but will give to your servant a male child, then I will set him before you as a nazirite until the day of his death. He shall drink neither wine nor intoxicants, and no razor shall touch his head." (1 Samuel 1:11-14)*
>
> *They rose early in the morning and worshiped before the Lord; then they went back to their house at Ramah. Elkanah knew his wife Hannah, and the Lord remembered her. In due time Hannah conceived and bore a son. She named him Samuel, for she said, "I have asked him of the Lord." (1 Samuel 1:19-20)*

Mothers, take a walk in Hannah's shoes. Reflect on your younger days when you wanted to have a baby. Think about the anticipation and excitement of being pregnant, especially since Hollywood glamorizes the entire process. Think about the prayers, the hopes, and the dreams you had for your precious bundle of joy. Think about how broken-hearted Hannah must have felt. She longed for a son, but could not have children.

Motherhood is a special privilege and a sacred duty. Hannah represents the multitude of women through the ages who deal with the agonizing experience of infertility or miscarriage. It's the deep and unsatisfied longing for children, the pain of watching others have babies, the pain of watching a mother kiss her newborn baby's perfect little face. But Hannah remained faithful and never gave up hope that God would hear her prayer. She was faithful even when Peninnah, Elkanah's other wife, taunted and provoked her because she was barren. Hannah wept and would not eat, but she remained steadfast in her faith. She even told God that if he blessed her with a son, she would dedicate her baby to the Lord and leave him at the temple to serve God "all the days of his life."

Hannah and I have a commonality. Although I did not wait as long as Hannah, I prayed for children, but to be very honest with you, I prayed for a little girl who would be just like me. I had big dreams of going to cute dance recitals, watching her play in my high heels and jewelry, dressing her in my sorority colors, and sending her to my alma mater, Spelman College. I could not wait to become her mother. After a year of marriage, we wanted to start a family, but I was unsuccessful. I prayed and prayed like Hannah. I tried to wager with God, *If you'll just let me get pregnant, God.*

When the doctor finally exclaimed "You are pregnant!", my excitement was similar to Hannah's. I had remained faithful and had not lost hope. God heard my prayer! However, I went into preterm labor and my baby did not survive. I was devastated.

I prayed and prayed some more, like Hannah did. I apologized to God for wanting a baby girl so badly that I cried when my first baby's ultrasound showed it was a boy. I tried to wager with God. *If you'll just let me get pregnant again, God, it's okay if it's a boy, I promise, I promise to be grateful.* I told God this, but in reality, I was 100% super girly girl. I didn't know anything about trucks, the color blue, or anything boy-related.

God heard my cry, and I became pregnant again. Due to complications with my first pregnancy, the doctor scheduled me for surgery so my baby would stay inside me, and I was on complete bed rest for six months. Baby boy Christian was born full-term and healthy.

About a year later, my sorority was deep into planning for our monumental 100th anniversary. I prayed again like Hannah. *Oh God, it's me again. Suppose you let me wager with you one more time. I would love to take my cute baby girl to my sorority's centennial celebration, so when she gets older and becomes a member, we will have pictures of us from the conference.* And guess what? I became pregnant, perfectly timed to take my baby girl to the 100-year celebration. Once again, my doctor scheduled me for surgery so my baby would stay inside of me, and I was on complete bed rest for another six months. And guess what? Baby boy Alexander was born full-term and healthy. God answers prayers and sometimes with a sense of humor.

God gave this girly girl two very active, jumping-off-the-couch little boys. Just like Hannah, I prayed and prayed. What am I going to do with these two bouncing boys? They liked trucks, Legos, sports, sneakers, video games, and all things boy. I have learned and grown. I know now more than I ever wanted to know about boy stuff. I am the mom who coordinated my sons' Cub Scouts pack. I can pitch a tent, watch football, shop for boy clothes, stay on top of the latest designer sneakers, listen to countless video game stories, and absolutely love being a boy mom!

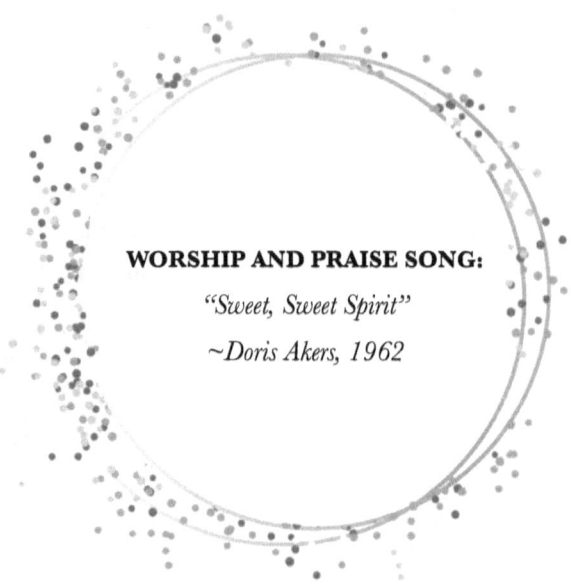

WORSHIP AND PRAISE SONG:

"Sweet, Sweet Spirit"

~Doris Akers, 1962

QUESTIONS:

1. Have you ever prayed like Hannah? When and what was the outcome?

2. This is Hannah's prayer. After reading and reflecting on it, write your own prayer to God.

Hannah's Prayer

· · · · · · · · · · · · · · · · · · ·

Hannah prayed and said,
"My heart exults in the Lord;
my strength is exalted in my God.
My mouth derides my enemies,
because I rejoice in my victory.
"There is no Holy One like the Lord,
no one besides you;
there is no Rock like our God.
Talk no more so very proudly,
let not arrogance come from your mouth;
for the Lord is a God of knowledge,
and by him actions are weighed.
The bows of the mighty are broken,
but the feeble gird on strength.
Those who were full have hired themselves out for bread,
but those who were hungry are fat with spoil.
The barren has borne seven,
but she who has many children is forlorn.
The Lord kills and brings to life;
he brings down to Sheol and raises up.
The Lord makes poor and makes rich;
he brings low, he also exalts.

He raises up the poor from the dust;
he lifts the needy from the ash heap,
to make them sit with princes
and inherit a seat of honor.
For the pillars of the earth are the Lord's,
and on them he has set the world.
"He will guard the feet of his faithful ones,
but the wicked shall be cut off in darkness;
for not by might does one prevail.
The Lord! His adversaries shall be shattered;
the Most High will thunder in heaven.
The Lord will judge the ends of the earth;
he will give strength to his king,
and exalt the power of his anointed."

(1 Samuel 2:1-10)

Chapter 2: You Don't Know My Story

There is a popular song by gospel recording artist John P. Kee, "Life & Favor (You Don't Know My Story)". The beginning lyrics say, "Some people have seen where God has brought you from. They don't really understand it. They don't know your story." Each of us has a story that God has intricately woven together to make us unique. My story makes me uniquely me, just as your story makes you uniquely you. When we are in relationship with God, not only do we have provision, but God supplies us with the strength we require for the journey ahead. Sometimes the journey ahead includes a detour that we never saw coming.

I worked in a large urban school system for 12 roller coaster years. Both exhilarating highs and devastating lows accompanied my positions as an elementary teacher and a school administrator. My goal was to be a principal, but the toxicity, bureaucracy, and nepotism in the school system lessened that desire.

While I was on track towards becoming a principal, the timing of my pregnancies and periods of bed rest were detrimental in my eyes, but both were in God's perfect timing. During the period of bed rest during my second pregnancy, my former husband came home one day and announced that God told him to quit his secular job to focus solely on his church. I was not bringing in any income because bed rest had already used up all of my available sick time. Therefore, we were operating on his secular job paycheck and his sporadic church paycheck. But after he quit his job, the church had to stop paying him due to financial constraints. At that point, we were living off credit cards and God's grace. Somehow, in the midst of it all, we were blessed to move into a beautiful new home.

After our baby was born, I was not permitted to return to work, even though I was cleared by the doctor. From September to June of that academic year, I was not paid. We existed on credit cards and his part-time consulting. I spent the following academic year trying to get caught up on late bills and mounting credit card debt.

As a new school term was beginning, I settled into the routine of another year of the same highs and lows. A friend told me about an open position at my undergraduate college that seemed like an absolute dream job. Thinking I wouldn't get hired because I was either not enough or not able to hold my own, I hesitated to apply. Michelle Obama discusses this concept of self-doubt and feeling like an imposter in her memoir, *Becoming*: "The messages that are sent from the time we are little is: maybe you are not, don't reach too high, don't talk too loud."

I forged ahead and applied for the position, as it was a perfect fit for my family and professional growth. There was one significant obstacle, though. The job paid $30,000 less than my current position. I had a serious talk with God. *How can I take this much of a pay cut, God? Why did you lead me to this position, God? What should I do, God?* After a few days of going back and forth in prayer, I accepted the position and was surprisingly at peace the moment I resigned from the school system. I absolutely loved my new job as director of the Marian Wright Edelman Center (formerly named Spelman College Nursery School and Kindergarten), which had a 78-year legacy on the campus. I was able to spend time doing what I loved and with my oldest son, who attended the school. My younger son would have been eligible to attend the following year.

About six weeks after taking the position, two things happened that caused my world to turn upside down.

I distinctly remember driving home one evening from work and picking my sons up from my parents' house. I was sitting at the closest traffic light to my home, which is known to have longer-than-usual wait times. To this day, it takes forever for the red light to turn green. While waiting at the red light for what seemed like an eternity, God revealed to me that my husband had cheated on me. I had not been thinking about the topic and, at that moment, was only focused on getting my sons home and preparing for the next day. Although our marriage was not perfect, surely God must have stopped by the wrong car at this long traffic light. My husband was running for public office and his church was growing. He would not be foolish enough to throw an opportunity for advancement and his family to the side for another woman.

As I drove through the gates of our subdivision, I saw my

husband. He was speaking to an unfamiliar woman. When I stopped to say hello, his demeanor was abrupt, demeaning, and unpleasant. When he came into the house soon after that, I asked who she was. His answer was short. Although he answered easily, his nasty attitude was resounding. Our evening continued as usual, with him retreating to his office.

Within a matter of days after that, my husband called and asked if I would come home before picking up the children. I arrived home and sat at the kitchen table. The conversation remains ingrained in my head and heart, but I will not recount the details. The conversation could have gone in another direction had I not been prepared by God's whisper at the traffic light. Yes, I was hurt, mad, and annoyed, but the wrath would have been different without my prior knowledge. In fact, my husband asked who told me before our conversation because my reaction was not what he expected. He could tell I had been forewarned, but he thought a family friend had shared the information. I never told him the source of information was *the* Source.

In the subsequent months that followed, we separated and I learned of more infidelity. I was conflicted about divorce, especially with two young boys. Although I met with a divorce attorney soon after learning about the infidelity, I carried the divorce papers in my work bag for six months before looking at them. In the sixth month of our separation, I became sick. I could not walk upright, had a urinary tract infection, and my blood pressure was at stroke level. I recall asking my husband to watch our baby, but he was too busy. I put my baby on the bed next to me, prayed he would be okay without supervision and that I would live through the night. The top number of my blood pressure was close to 200 before I went to sleep. The next day, I contacted my lawyer and proceeded with the divorce. When I eventually filed, while it was not an easy decision, it was one that was accomplished through fervent prayer, daily tears and meltdowns, and counseling sessions.

The journey to forgiving my former husband for his infidelity has not been easy. Even reading my old journal entries to write this book brings back old wounds that now feel fresh again. The memories bring back old emotions and tears. The memories bring back feelings of worthlessness and being called a liar for merely presenting the truth.

I cannot walk in my truth and minister to readers by lying. The hurt was real. The hurt was raw. Forgiving him was not easy.

Life was difficult during the divorce and in the years that followed. My paycheck did not cover the bills. There were many days I did not have enough money in my bank account for a carton of milk. I couldn't pay my mortgage. My car kept breaking down. Every time I had it fixed, a new problem would pop up, and I ended up driving it to the bank and leaving the keys in the night deposit box. I was paying weekly daycare fees for my youngest son. I was drowning in credit card debt from having to pay bills with credit cards.

I had to move out of my beautiful home and away from my wonderful neighbors. It was such an embarrassing and humiliating experience, but some of my neighbors prayed for and with me. My next-door neighbors always had an encouraging word and a prayer. They allowed me to see the blessings in my life and told me everything would be alright.

I ended up moving four times in three years. It was an awful time. My boys were frustrated and confused. I was frustrated and beat down.

I have seen the negative effects of divorce on my two sons. When I reflect on our three rounds of marriage counseling, which we both got two totally different viewpoints about, I wonder how life would have been if we were still married. Whenever I have a doubt, my relationship with God always confirms my prayerful decision.

When I learned of my former husband's infidelity, I was devastated and spent the majority of my workdays in a daze. I didn't know if I was coming or going. The concept of divorce was not in my life plan, but here it was, staring me in the face.

The second major blow came just a matter of days after my husband confirmed his infidelity. The college president announced her desire to close the Marian Wright Edelman Center. Several attempts by the beloved Center's Parent-Teacher Association to keep it open were met with opposition. Between my looming divorce and the impending loss of my job, I thought I would lose my sanity.

However, through prayer, I also realized a blessing during this tumultuous time. I had peace in my workplace. Every day I drove through the college's gates, I had peace. I knew I was in the right place at that moment in my life. Had I stayed at my previous job, with its nonstop stress and multiple simultaneously-moving parts, I would not have been able to process a stressful job and a devastating marital situation at the same time. God brings blessings when we follow God's lead.

Hard times are unavoidable, but how we handle them reveals a deeper layer of who we are and what we care about most. If we are too busy feeling sorry for ourselves, we miss out on the opportunity to learn from our challenges and valley moments. Challenging situations take us beyond our comfort zone, keep us on our toes, and have the power to become moments of truth. Challenges can be the ultimate lesson we learn about ourselves.

Yes, I have experienced sad days, tough financial crises, and difficult changes, but God always provides for my needs and lights my path with favor. When God lights your path with favor and gives you steadfast confirmation, walk on, sister, walk on.

CHAPTER 2: DEVOTION

Create in me a clean heart, O God, and put a new and right spirit within me.
(Psalm 51:10)

Sometimes one's appearance does not match his or her reality. I am reminded of an encounter in a summer Vacation Bible School class. When I arrived at the church, I came dressed in a tennis skirt and an athletic top. My hair was in a high ponytail. A participant's skewed perception of me caused her to look down on me and speak to me in a condescending tone of voice. At this point in the conversation, I did not know her perception of me. All I knew was that she was speaking to me in a condensing tone whenever I attempted to answer a question.

The next evening, the participant pulled me to the side and profusely apologized. She explained that a church member who knew me well had shared my story with her. She assumed that I was a teenager with an inappropriate short skirt on at church. Also, because my boys are two different skin tones, one has a chocolate complexion and the other is caramel, in her mind, I was a teenage mother with children from different fathers.

I was not wearing an inappropriate short skirt to Vacation Bible School; I was heading to a tennis match after the evening session. While my ponytail may have made me look like a teenager, I was over

40, a professor at a well-respected college, and a divorced woman. In addition, my sons have the same father and their skin colors are like many families in the Black community—a representation of the generations.

The woman had erroneously misjudged me, and her perception of me affected her conversation with me. I did forgive her, but this encounter has always bothered me. Why does it matter what someone's background is, to be treated with respect? Why did it matter what I was wearing to Vacation Bible School? Why did it matter what I looked like to learn the Word of God?

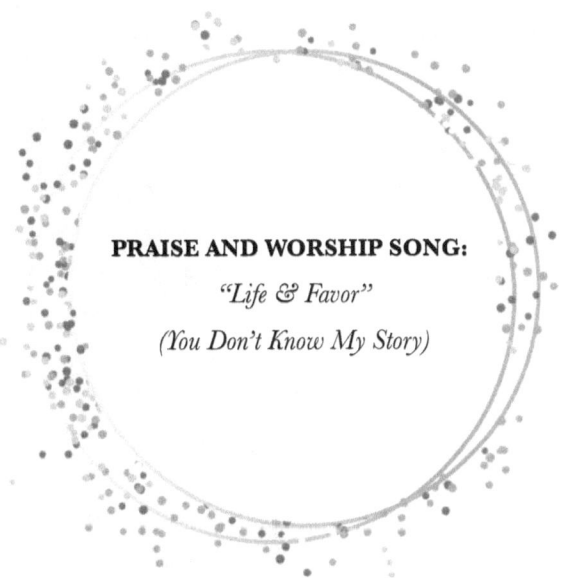

PRAISE AND WORSHIP SONG:

"Life & Favor"

(You Don't Know My Story)

QUESTIONS

1. Has your bias or perception of someone led you to misjudge his or her reality?

2. How did you handle the situation?

3. Has someone else's bias or perception of you led to misjudgment?

4. How did you handle the situation?

5. How can we work on looking at someone's heart before their appearance?

Chapter 3: Peace, Be Still

Mark 4:35-41 tells the story of Jesus and His disciples on a boat one stormy evening, on their way to minister to the people. They were exhausted.

The passages state:

> On that day, when evening had come, he said to them, "Let us go across to the other side." And leaving the crowd behind, they took him with them in the boat, just as he was. Other boats were with him. A great windstorm arose, and the waves beat into the boat, so that the boat was already being swamped. But he was in the stern, asleep on the cushion; and they woke him up and said to him, "Teacher, do you not care that we are perishing?" He woke up and rebuked the wind, and said to the sea, "Peace! Be still!" Then the wind ceased, and there was a dead calm. He said to them, "Why are you afraid? Have you still no faith?" And they were filled with great awe and said to one another, "Who then is this, that even the wind and the sea obey him?"

When I was younger, my parents had a record player cabinet. I'm sure it had a fancy name, but I knew it as the large piece of furniture where we could stack multiple vinyl records on the player and play the songs in random order. It sounds odd to the new generation, but I used to watch the needle adjust as the records changed, then glide across the record slowly as music came out like magic. In the rotation, there was always a James Cleveland album. The song "Peace Be Still" played almost daily. Reverend Cleveland sang, "The winds and the waves shall obey my will, peace be still."

As the boat left the shore, the lake was calm. I imagine beautiful blue skies and serenity as the boat glided across the water. Jesus decided to go to sleep in the rear of the boat. Seemingly from nowhere, a raging storm arose over the lake. The wind and the waves caused the boat to rock and pitch. As the raging water crashed into the boat, the disciples worked feverishly to save themselves and keep the boat from taking in the increasing water. After a period of turmoil and desperation, the disciples woke up Jesus. They asked a question that may seem inappropriate to ask someone as divine as Jesus, but I believe it is a question we have all asked at least once in our lives, "Teacher, don't you care if we drown?"

In the midst of our tumultuous storms in life, I would imagine that our 21st century questions would include:

Teacher, don't you care if my marriage falls apart?

Teacher, don't you care that my father is suffering from cancer?

Teacher, don't you care that I can't pay my mortgage?

Teacher, don't you care that I can't make my car payment?

Teacher, don't you care that I can't pay daycare?

Teacher, don't you care that I can't focus on my dissertation?

Teacher, don't you care that I can't buy my textbooks this

semester?

Teacher, don't you care that I can't breathe – there's a knee on my neck?

Teacher, don't you care that I am drowning in pain?

Teacher, don't you care?

Teacher?

I know we have all prayed and asked God questions like these throughout our lives, especially during the most trying times. When I was going through my storm, I asked God the questions above almost daily, sometimes hourly. I was drowning in pain. I was drowning in debt. I was drowning in fear. I did not have peace, so I could not be still.

When Jesus woke up from the disciples' nervous noise, He spoke three words, "Peace! Be still." And if I could at this moment, I would queue James Cleveland on that old-fashioned record player. To the disciples, Jesus said, "Why are you so afraid? Have you still no faith?" Like the disciples on the boat, I had lost my faith and my way.

Yes, the disciples had faith in Jesus. They believed in Him because their faith was ingrained in their minds and souls. I had lost my faith, even though it was ingrained in my mind and soul from childhood. Some Sundays I would go to church, but not be in a church frame of mind. I went because I knew that was where I was supposed to be. I opened my Bible because I knew I was supposed to open it, but the words did not speak to me. I prayed, but the words were automatic and did not come from the heart. I was in a storm, the waves were overflowing into my boat, and I was drowning.

I remember driving to church one Sunday with my boys, but somehow ended up at Chuck E. Cheese instead. I was in a dress and my boys were in suits. Since it was so early, we were the only family in the building, so my boys jumped and played while I cried at a table. On this day, I pulled myself together because my boys could not continue to see a mother with a broken spirit. Through the ministry of Chuck E. Cheese, pizza, and soda, I decided to ask Jesus to take me out of my storm.

I recall a sermon on the Keep Believing Ministries website that referenced the concept of storms in our lives and who led the disciples to the storm. When we have storms in our lives, finding a way through the wind and the waves is easier said than done. We have to climb in the boat and ride through the storm with Jesus. He will hold your hand and give you the strength you need to make it to the other side. Jesus is the ultimate ride or die, through thick and thin. He is with us during the good times and the bad.

Let's go back to the first point, which is a game-changer when we reflect on Jesus' love and divinity. Jesus told the disciples to get into the boat and ride to the other side of the lake. Did Jesus know about the pending storm? Absolutely. Jesus knows when your storm is coming. Should Jesus have warned the disciples? Absolutely not. Should Jesus tap you on the shoulder and say your storm is coming? Absolutely not. Jesus equipped us with the word and knowledge of God's promises to guide us through trying times. Jesus had already worked out the disciples' storm. Jesus has already worked out your storm, even when you feel alone.

When life caves in all around us, even when we have tried to serve God to the best of our ability, there are times when we feel God has left us. Who knows that feeling? I think we have all felt it at one time or another.

In these moments, we have choices to make that can get us through the journey. We can choose to believe that God sent the storm to us for a reason or season, or we can choose to believe that God has abandoned us.

I do not believe God leaves us alone. If anything, this parable teaches the opposite. At times, our path takes us into the storm, and at other times we see the storm brewing. When the winds rise and the waves rage and our lives turn upside down, Jesus has control over it all. When He calls us, like the disciples, we get into the boat. When the storm pours down on us, we pray and cry out to Jesus. When He responds, He calms the storm and allays our fears. And, when the storm is over, our faith looks up to Him. We grow stronger in our faith, in our capacity to trust, and in His Word.

God's lessons are not only in the overwhelming problems of life, but sometimes they are in the simple and mundane minutes of the day.

Let God's peace fill your heart right now. Even if you do not feel it, you are in God's loving embrace at this very moment. God will strengthen and keep you. Just put your hand in God's hand, and God will say, "Peace be still."

CHAPTER 3: DEVOTION

The Lord bless you and keep you; the Lord make his face to shine upon you, and be gracious to you; the Lord lift up his countenance upon you, and give you peace. (Numbers 6:24-26)

During a visit to Animal Kingdom in Walt Disney World, my boys and a friend's son wanted to go on Avatar Flight of Passage, the flagship ride in a new section of the park modeled after the fictitious planet Pandora. It was a holiday weekend, so the lines were long. It was also raining. The sign said the wait was 105 minutes, but somehow in our delirious and rain-soaked state of mind, my friend and I both understood that to mean one hour and five minutes. After standing in the line for that long and finding that there was still no end in sight to our wait, we became confused and tired. A crew member had to explain to us that it wasn't an hour and five minutes but 105 minutes. Which meant we still had 40 more minutes to go!

This represents the part of the story in Mark, when the boat starts rocking. We were looking for a way out, but there was nowhere to go, so we had to stand and wait. When we finally made it to the beginning of the Avatar ride, it was not what I expected. My children know I'm not too fond of roller coasters or anything that resembles a roller coaster. But here I was, hoodwinked once again at an amusement park. The Avatar was a *virtual* roller coaster, which to me is just as bad as a real one. The winds were really starting to kick up for me now, and I really would have liked to get off that boat already. Nevertheless, we put on our 3D glasses, and then the ride started.

I couldn't see my boys even though they were sitting next to me. It was pitch black except for the screen that simulated us flying through the land of Pandora. The Avatars were jumping out in our faces. We were flying up and down and dipping and swerving back and forth. Everyone on the ride with us was screaming. The music was so loud. I was strapped in my seat and could not move. *Teacher, don't you care that I'm about to die on this ride?*

This is when Jesus calmed the storm. I closed my eyes and tuned out the noise. I started meditating right there on the ride. I thought about how God protects us through the storms of life. I thought about Jesus calming the storm. I kept my eyes closed, relaxed my body, and focused on peace. When the ride was over, my boys could not believe I wasn't afraid. They said they didn't hear me scream. They were so excited, telling me about all they experienced in Pandora and could not understand why I had not seen it all too. They did not understand that I chose peace over Pandora.

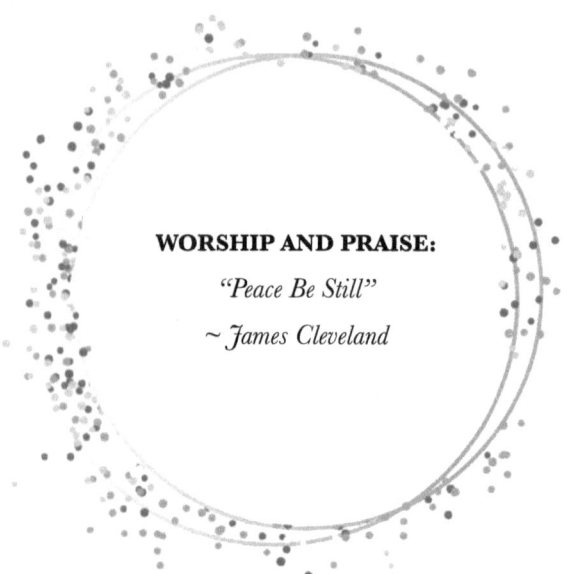

WORSHIP AND PRAISE:

"Peace Be Still"

~ James Cleveland

QUESTIONS

1. What is disrupting your peace?

2. How can you find more 'me time' in your life to experience peace and God's voice?

3. What question would you ask Jesus as the boat was sinking? "Teacher, don't you care that _____?"

Chapter 4: Cast Your Net

After these things Jesus showed himself again to the disciples by the Sea of Tiberias; and he showed himself in this way. Gathered there together were Simon Peter, Thomas called the Twin, Nathanael of Cana in Galilee, the sons of Zebedee, and two others of his disciples. Simon Peter said to them, "I am going fishing." They said to him, "We will go with you." They went out and got into the boat, but that night they caught nothing.

Just after daybreak, Jesus stood on the beach; but the disciples did not know that it was Jesus. Jesus said to them, "Children, you have no fish, have you?" They answered him, "No." He said to them, "Cast the net to the right side of the boat, and you will find some." So they cast it, and now they were not able to haul it in because there were so many fish. (John 21:1-6)

On April 11, 1881, two White missionaries from New England, Sophia B. Packard and Harriet E. Giles, opened Atlanta Baptist Female Seminary in the basement of Friendship Baptist Church with one hundred dollars and ten women and one girl, most of whom were formerly enslaved. The legacy of Atlanta Baptist Female Seminary, which was renamed Spelman

Seminary and then Spelman College, is one of academic excellence, social justice, and global engagement.

Like the disciples in John 21:1-6, I decided to follow God from an early age. And, God has always shown me where to cast my net. When I was in sixth grade, God told me to attend Spelman College. I cannot explain the "why," but I knew I had to get there from my home state of New Jersey. Throughout my middle and high school years, that was my one goal and I worked hard to fulfill it.

When I visited Spelman during my junior year of high school and went through those campus gates for the first time, the feeling was indescribable. It was like a sense of peace and belonging came over me. I was centered. I was at home.

When it came time to apply during the fall of my senior year, I asked for no help from my parents and paid the application fee myself from my job. I was over-the-top excited when I received my letter of acceptance, which arrived before Christmas. I thought my college application process was complete until my mom asked where else I was applying. After I replied "nowhere", she immediately made me apply to several other schools. I received scholarship money at every institution, including a full four-year academic scholarship to a university in New Jersey. That sealed the deal for my mom. She made me attend orientation there, take my placement tests, and meet my roommate.

I could not verbally express to my mom in words that God told me to go to Spelman. Spelman, the school that offered me zero dollars in financial aid as opposed to the opportunity to attend another university for free. I believe my dad sensed God working in my life. We had family discussion after discussion, but my mom was not budging. My spirit was crushed. But, behind the scenes, my dad paid my deposit at Spelman. I think he knew that my laser focus on Spelman was coming from God. In the end, my mom consented, and in August 1992, I arrived in Atlanta. When I walked through those gates as a freshwoman, that feeling came back. I felt a sense of peace and belonging. I was centered. I was at home.

As I said, I received no scholarship offers from Spelman College. Fortunately, after I started with funds my parents had been saving, I received a scholarship each year from the DeWitt Wallace Reader's Digest Fund. I graduated with zero dollars in debt and a fully paid-off bill. I also graduated summa cum laude and with a job secured in the local school system.

The point of my sharing this accomplishment is that God told me where to cast my net even as a sixth grader. God showed me the side of the boat to cast my net from, and he poured out financial resources to make it happen. God did not show my parents. God showed me. It was my battle to fight. I had to get and maintain good grades in middle and high school. I had to stay out of trouble. I had to earn a Scholastic Assessment Test (SAT) score worthy of college admissions. God gave me the direction and I had to pull my net over to catch my blessing.

When God speaks to you and gives you direction, follow God. Do not doubt. God will make it happen. If you cannot afford it, God will make a way. If God brought you to it, God will bring you through it.

The disciples did not ask the who, what, when, where, and how of getting the net to the other side of the boat. They just did it. They moved the net. They adjusted their plans. And God made a way through Jesus Christ. God will continue to do the same for you.

When I went through my divorce and financial challenges, I had to listen to God and let my Creator cast my net. God set me on a professional and personal journey when I was led into a period of decrease. When I was hired at Spelman College to lead the nursery school, I had big plans to expand the center to include an elementary school. The school's Parent-Teacher Association (PTA) had plans to expand extracurricular activities and strengthen recruiting. No matter how much we worked together, envisioning a bigger and better center, our plans were not the college president's plans. The president announced that the center was closing, and regardless of the efforts of the parents and staff, the 79-year legacy of the center ended.

After that, I transitioned to full-time teaching at the college and also completed my doctorate. Since my background was in the public school system, I had to quickly learn the landscape of higher education. The thought of attaining tenure and publishing academic scholarship sounded daunting, but in addition to my faith, the words to my alma mater's hymn, "undaunted by the fight", kept my eyes focused on the task ahead. In my quest to earn tenure, I wrote scholarly articles and book chapters, and still to my amazement, published three books with God's help.

After settling into higher education, I became frustrated because a new supervisor made each day a challenge. It took 30 minutes or more to get out of my car every morning because I knew there would be no peace once I entered my workspace. After going on a few interviews in search of a new job, I received an offer to return to the school system. The prospect of a new opportunity away from my supervisor and to earn more money sounded like a blessing; however, whenever I prayed about leaving my job, God's voice always said no. In my secular reasoning, the job sounded perfect, but God still said no.

During this same time, my dad was nearing the end of his life. The cancer, which had gone into remission, had returned, and his resolve for life was diminishing. He no longer wanted to fight. On one of my final visits with him, he asked what was wrong. I shared my new job opportunity. Even though he knew my struggles at work and also loved the principal who hired me, my dad told me to stay in my job. "Listen to God," he told me.

After my conversation with my dad, I reflected on one of my favorite scriptures, Isaiah 30:21 which says, "And when you turn to the right or when you turn to the left, your ears shall hear a word behind you, saying, 'This is the way; walk in it.'" I had my answer. God's voice was telling me to stay. Less than three months later, I replaced my supervisor and established a spirit of peace and respect in our department. This season of my life was a reminder to always listen to God. When God tells us where to cast our net, God will guide the way. God will never let us down.

In all that you may be going through, let God direct your way. In order for this to happen, you must open your heart, ears, and mind to God's voice. Let God cast your net. Let God fill your net with so many blessings that you will have trouble hauling it in because of the overwhelming number of blessings. Be led by God. God will never leave you or forsake you.

QUESTIONS

1. In your transition from plan A to plan B, where is God telling you to cast your net?

2. Are you open or have you blocked God's direction of where to cast your net?

3. How can you be more open to God's will as you transition journeys?

Chapter 5: When Plan 'A' Fails

Sometimes when plan A fails, we think we are a failure. Many girls are raised to have a plan. We plan which college we will attend, which organizations we will join, what career we will have, how old we will be when we get married, how many bridesmaids we will have, how many children we will have, when we will move to a bigger house, when we will retire… the list is endless. Our plans are usually not God's plans. Our plans are rigid and do not allow for changes. But when we give our lives to God, we have to get out of our own way.

Girls are raised to have everything in order and to be mature. Marginalized girls are taught that they must work two times harder to climb the professional ladder. When I attended college, expectations were high. At many colleges during new student orientation, students are told, "Look to your right, look to your left. Those people may not be sitting next to you on graduation day." At my undergraduate institution, our Sister President Johnnetta Betsch Cole, who led with grace, charisma, sisterhood, and regal authority, put it this way - Look to your right, look to your left. Make sure those sisters are sitting next to you on graduation day. There was an expectation to nurture our village of classmates. Another expectation was to live up to the college's reputation and legacy of excellence.

When I was going through my struggles, I felt that I failed that legacy. I was not high achieving and high performing during those moments in life. What I had to realize was that I was still a Spelman woman because I preserved through the storm and made it through to the dry land. I struggled, but I conquered. I fell, but I got back up. I think back to those first 11 students at Atlanta Baptist Female Seminary on April 11, 1881. Many of the women had been enslaved, but that was not their destiny. They persevered and received an education. They were the first alumnae of the institution now known as Spelman College.

Besides those first students who paved the way, I thought about other graduates in the college's history. How many of them divorced, overcame sickness, conquered financial struggles, and survived insurmountable odds? I am positive that the number is more than a handful. I am also positive that there are millions of women across the globe who hide their struggles privately for fear of a failed plan A. Sometimes plan A is not God's plan for us. God does not desire for us to be unfulfilled, unhappy, or unmotivated. *For surely I know the plans I have for you, says the Lord, plans for your welfare and not for harm, to give you a future with hope.* (Jeremiah 29:11).

When I was in sixth grade, I thought I knew. I knew what college I wanted to attend. I knew what age I wanted to get married. I knew I wanted to marry a basketball player. I knew I wanted a daughter. I knew I wanted to be a principal. The only plan that came true was the college I attended, and it was a struggle to get there.

After all these disappointments, I asked God what I did wrong. What I have come to realize is that I did not do anything wrong. You did not do anything wrong. The lesson learned is that our plan A may not be in God's plan for us. Am I a failure because I am not an elementary school principal? No, it means that God had other plans for my life. Proverbs 19:21 reminds us, *Many are the plans in a person's heart, but it is the Lord's purpose that prevails.* We make grandiose plans for our life, but God's purpose and plans for us will always prevail. When plan A fails, life is not over.

In the Union Theological Seminary video "Journey to Liberation: The Legacy of Womanist Theology," Rev. Dr. Katie Geneva Cannon shared these poignant words:

> *"Everybody has a vocation and you don't leave this life until you finish the work God has called you to do. And, some people go sooner than others, but everybody has a call on your life. And part of your responsibility as a Christian...was to find out what is God calling you to do. What's the work your soul must have so that you can live a faithful life and a full life?"*

If you are not living the faithful and full life that your soul must have, use the following 15 guidelines that I created to persevere and redefine your life with God's grace. The corresponding devotions to these guidelines are located after Chapter 7.

1. STOP AND LOCATE YOUR BREATH, STOP AND LOCATE YOUR HURT

The Lord will fight for you, and you have only to keep still.
(Exodus 14:14)

The most important step in overcoming a challenge is to take a pause. Many times, when life confronts us with a curve ball, we activate our senses into high gear. We go into emergency mode. We want to confront the problem, often without a plan. We have not even stopped to find out the who, what, when, where, and how of what happened. We are in overdrive to get to the next step without even stopping, catching our breath, finding out what is wrong, and then making a plan. You have to find out where your pain is located. What is the source of your pain? Locate it—is it your marriage, the loss of a career, your health, financial crisis, becoming a caretaker, or a loved one's death? Whatever is derailing your plan A, pinpoint it first. Do not go into overdrive without cause.

When my marriage was falling apart, I was quick to contact an attorney and secure the appropriate paperwork. I moved out of my house one Saturday morning when my husband was at a church meeting. I never stopped to catch my breath.

Similarly, when someone close to us passes away, we immediately start making arrangements and catering to others. We rarely stop to catch our breath. And, in these trying times, we not only have to catch our breath, but we have to locate our breath. We have to center ourselves and find our hurt. I had to figure out why I wanted a divorce. Why was I hurt? Could I work through the infidelity and stay in my marriage?

I paused my deliberations, moved back into my house, went to counseling, sought the advice of other married and divorced women who experienced infidelity in their marriages, and prayed many prayers, then I proceeded.

Sometimes we do not stop long enough to feel the pain because we are too busy trying to work the pain away. Take a moment to stop, locate your breath, and locate your hurt.

2. LET GO AND LET GOD

Cast your burden on the Lord, and he will sustain you; he will never permit the righteous to be moved. (Psalm 55:22)

Once you locate your pain, let it go and give it to God. This is often much easier said than done, especially because some people view it as a cliché expression. But it is the truth. Give God your problems, especially those you do not have control over. When you pray, tell God your troubles and leave them at the altar. When you turn your problems over to God, you must be willing to submit to God's will for your life. God will see you through this difficult season, in God's perfect timing. However, God's will may not be the answer you desired. It may be better!

Isaiah 55: 8-9 reminds us, *For my thoughts are not your thoughts, nor are your ways my ways, says the Lord. For as the heavens are higher than the earth, so are my ways higher than your ways and my thoughts than your thoughts.* Give it to God because God will always work it out for you.

3. PRAY

Then you will call upon me and come and pray to me, and I will hear you. (Jeremiah 29:12)

After you give the pain to God, pray. Pray unceasingly, because God has you in a sweet and protective embrace. Be encouraged in the comfort of God, but be reminded that God will answer in God's perfect timing, not your preferred timing. Pray, read, and listen to God's Word. Pray and ground yourself in God's Word. Pray and center yourself in God's grace. Be encouraged by God's promises outlined in the Bible. Be uplifted through praise and worship. Be renewed by gathering with like-minded believers.

While you take in God's Word, recall the parable of the mustard seed in Mathew 17:20: *He said to them, "Because of your little faith. For truly I tell you, if you have faith the size of a mustard seed, you will say to this mountain, 'Move from here to there,' and it will move; and nothing will be impossible for you."* Stay prayed up and keep your faith up. God will see you through to brighter days

4. LISTEN TO YOU, YOU KNOW WHAT YOU NEED

I will instruct you and teach you the way you should go; I will counsel you with my eye upon you. (Psalm 32:8)

Sometimes, members of our sister circles jump into overdrive to come to our rescue. They mean well, and we need our sister friends, but there comes a point where you have to listen to *you*. When we are going through a storm, those around us want to offer advice based on what they have been through. Sis, listen to your inner voice. You know you. What do you need? Often, you do not need a multitude of people around you in your ear. You do not need to hear what everyone else went through. You do not need another food delivery. You do not need another homemade cake. You do not need another gift basket. You do not need more wine. You do not need any more flowers or bubble bath products. You need to escape from the noise and listen to you.

Maybe you need a getaway to the beach to be soothed by the ocean's waves, or to the mountains to feel the crisp breeze. God speaks to us through the ocean's waves and cool breeze. Maybe you need your favorite comfort food while you curl up on your sofa. God speaks to us in the silence. Whatever you need, you know what it is; however, it's not something that will harm you or cause you to backslide into overindulgence, abuse, or addiction.

5. RETREAT

And after he had dismissed the crowds, he went up the mountain by himself to pray. When evening came, he was there alone.
(Matthew 14:23)

When Jesus was overwhelmed, He went to the mountains for prayer in solitude. You need to do the same. Retreat from the noise and all the people around you. Take time to unplug from the world, retreat, and cleanse your mind. When major life forces derail your plans, take time to center yourself and be still. You have to step away and rejuvenate your mind, body, and spirit to become one with God's will for your life.

If you can afford it, take a vacation to a favorite destination or somewhere you have longed to go. Enjoy the sun, beach, mountains, cool air, whatever it is that you will enjoy. If you do not have enough money to travel, consider a staycation in your city or town. A change in your daily scenery will be good for you to pray, process, and move forward.

6. REFLECT

So if anyone is in Christ, there is a new creation: everything old has passed away; see, everything has become new! (2 Corinthians 5:17)

As you retreat, reflect on what went wrong, if anything. Why didn't you get that promotion? Why didn't you get accepted to an organization or graduate school? Why is my family not speaking to me? After reflecting, you may realize that the issue was out of your control. Sometimes God closes a door to make way for blessings. Sometimes God closes a door to protect you from physical, emotional, or financial harm. If the situation was out of your control, keep moving onto your plan B. There is no point in wallowing in pity when it is out of your hands.

If you realize you were the cause of the demise of your plan A, think about what change you can make as you move into your plan B. Do you need to center yourself back to God? Ask for forgiveness? Change your attitude? Work on your personality? Take inventory of the company you keep?

7. BE REALISTIC

Do not be conformed to this world, but be transformed by the renewal of your mind, that by testing you may discern what is the will of God, what is good and acceptable and perfect. (Romans 12:2)

As you maneuver in your new normal, learn to be realistic and patient with yourself. You may not be able to afford or go to the places you used to go. You may not be able to travel or make the same purchases. You may have to live with less. You may have to relocate or rely on others for transportation. You may have to rely on others for physical or financial help. Being realistic allows you to center yourself in a new normal.

8. BE OPEN TO CHANGE

Put away from you all bitterness and wrath and anger and wrangling

and slander, together with all malice, and be kind to one another,
tenderhearted, forgiving one another, as God in Christ has forgiven you.
(Ephesians 4:31-32)

In being realistic, be open to change. You may experience a loss of things—co-workers, family, independence, or something else. Without change, change cannot happen. You may have to change for change to happen. Change your pace, change your attitude, change your location, change your mindset, change your company, change your finances, and who knows what else. You may have to lose something in your move to plan B.

9. DO NOT BE AFRAID TO ASK FOR HELP

God is within her, she will not fall; God will help her at break of day.
(Psalm 46:5 NIV)

As you are going through the storms and valleys of life, seek help from mental health professionals, church leaders, and brothers and sisters in Christ. Sometimes people come into our lives because God told them to help you. Be accepting of their help, if it seems genuine.

Sometimes, in our new temporary normal, we have to ask for help. For some of us, including me, asking for help is the most difficult thing to do. But it can be the catalyst to moving to the next phase of life. The person who responds when you ask could have a job opportunity, help with a bill, or assistance with a car or clothes. Whatever it is, ask, and it shall be given to you.

10. DO NOT BE EMBARRASSED

Cast all your anxiety on him, because he cares for you. (1 Peter 5:7)

If you are like me, asking for help can be embarrassing, but don't let it be. Everyone faces hard times, and you have to push past the embarrassment of loss. Loss of income, loss of a relationship, loss of mobility, loss of a home—whatever it is, be resilient because life happens.

11. KEEP YOUR CIRCLE TIGHT

Perfume and incense bring joy to the heart, and the pleasantness of a friend springs from their heartfelt advice. (Proverbs 27:9 NIV)

When you are going through the valley, it's okay to ask for help, but not everyone needs to know the details of your troubles. Not everyone needs to be familiar with the intricacies of your late payments, diagnosis, family drama, or loss of finances, because not everyone is rooting for you. Keep your friend circle tight to include those who are supportive and mean you well.

People will run and tell your business, but if you do not give them any business to tell, they can't run and tell it! Guard your troubles and stay within your friend circle.

12. TAKE CARE OF YOURSELF

Do you not know that you are God's temple and that God's Spirit dwells in you? (1 Corinthians 3:16)

As you transition to your plan B, give yourself grace and patience to fail. It is a part of the overcoming process. When you get back on top, which you will, you don't want to look like what you've been through. In the interim, find something that you enjoy—fitness, travel, the spa, music, long baths—whatever you can take the time to do to make your joy a priority. When you are going through stuff, do something to take care of you.

13. BUILD YOUR SECONDARY SKILL SET

For this very reason, you must make every effort to support your faith with goodness, and goodness with knowledge. (2 Peter 1:5)

Always make sure you have a secondary skill set, also known as a side hustle. When hard times come, you may need to fall back on your side hustle for income or even experience.

A hobby or side hustle skill set allows you to keep the bills paid as you move into plan B. And, for some, your side hustle may turn into your plan B.

14. PUT ONE FOOT IN FRONT OF THE OTHER AND WALK IN YOUR NEW DESTINY

All our steps are ordered by the LORD; how then can we understand our own ways. (Proverbs 20:24)

After you have conquered numbers 1-13, do not look back. Do not be like Lot's wife, who looked back and turned into a pillar of salt. Keep looking ahead, and focus on the new you. A new career, a new job, a renewed sense of peace as a single woman, increased finances, improved health, plan for caretaking—whatever you are creating for your plan B, put one foot in front of the other. That is how you start. One step at a time, sis.

15. OWN THE GAME YOU WANT TO WIN

No one after lighting a lamp puts it under the bushel basket, but on the lampstand, and it gives light to all in the house. (Matthew 5:15)

Slay
Just do it
Be lit
Be poppin'
Get your glow on
Kill it

Depending on your generational slang and however you say it, walk into your plan B in a big way! Do it with a smile. What I have found is that sometimes your plan B is really what you were supposed to be doing in the first place, instead of plan A. Plan B should have been your plan A to begin with.

Take advantage of every opportunity you are given, even if it seems trivial at the moment. Receive God's blessings, because you do not know where they may lead you.

Walk in God's favor, live in God's glory, and do it big in God's name.

When I was in the valley, I could not allow my sons to see a broken mother. These 15 steps became my mantra for rising up and out of the chaos. There comes a point when you have to face the facts and close the door on your plan A. Honestly, maybe plan A was not your God-ordained plan. God allowed it, but God may not have ordained it.

We have to rewind, readjust, reshuffle, and regroup. Let God handle it all while you work on yourself. Keep pressing and pushing. That is the beauty of your story: you will overcome. You may be down for the count. You may have hit rock bottom. Readjust; you can do it. I know you can! Stay undaunted! There will be battles out there, but your setback is a setup for your comeback!

Chapter 6: God's Plan

Embracing God's will for our lives can be difficult when we want to lead instead of allowing God to guide. Proverbs 3:6 says, "In all your ways acknowledge him, and he will make straight your paths." Sometimes we acknowledge God as the head of our lives, but do not allow God to lead. In those times, our paths are not straight. Instead, the paths lead all over the place, but not to God.

Sometimes we live our entire lives this way. Sometimes, we don't surrender our *entire* being to God. For me, it was the latter. I gave God part of me, but not the part God was calling. For years, I ran from God's call on my life, but I also felt like I could live my call through my dad and my former husband, who were both pastors. I knew the call was there, but I bargained with God. *God, if you let me have children. God, if you let me get through this divorce. God, if you let me finish my doctoral degree. God, if you let me get adjusted to a new job. God, if you let me get through caretaking. God, if you let me get through this next thing.* And the long list of *"God, if you let me"* continued through the years until I finally stopped running.

In the African Methodist Episcopal (AME) denomination, the

ordination process includes going through the Board of Examiners (BOE). The BOE is composed of experienced pastors who teach and mentor candidates through the ordination process over the course of five years. In the admissions year, a lot of focus and discussion is on one's call story. Several of my classmates could pinpoint the exact moment they were called by God. However, I have known since childhood that I was called to ministry.

As a child, I didn't know how to frame the understanding, but as I grew up, I recognized it as God's call on my life. When I began reading for a seminary assignment, the first page of Chapter 1 in *Recalling Our Own Stories: Spiritual Renewal for Religious Caregivers* by Dr. Edward P. Wimberly, the words I had been searching for hit me like a ton of bricks. What I had been trying to vocalize in BOE was right before my eyes. It said, "Generally, most of us in ministry can identify the point in our lives at which we can say we made a commitment to ministry."[1] For me, I know that I was called by God to do his work, but Wimberly's book made it plain.

I knew I was called by God a long time ago, but I kept fighting it to complete my professional and personal endeavors. God kept knocking, and I kept ignoring. For all the years I ran from my calling, I never told my dad. We had conversations about God, but never about my call to ministry.

As a young child, my dad told me that I had to speak at his funeral. From time to time, usually at odd times, he would remind me of my charge to speak at his funeral. When he became ill, he reminded me again. So when the time came, I fulfilled my dad's request. And, at that moment as I was speaking at his funeral, something came over me. When I thought I would be unable to speak, God allowed the words to pour out, and I could feel the Holy Spirit upon me.

Next to God and family, my dad's next love was the sport of track and field. He ran track as a child and in high school. Every year until his health failed, my dad attended the Penn Relays, the United States' oldest and largest track and field competition that is held annually at the University of Pennsylvania. Even our family had to endure sitting in the hot sun for track and field events. During the 1996 Summer Olympics in Atlanta my dad was totally in his element during those scorching hot days. His favorite event was the relay race, in which runners passed a baton to the next team member after completing their portion of the race. He often spoke in metaphors about passing the baton.

Fast-forward seven years after my dad's funeral, I was reading the text by Dr. Wimberly. As I read these words, I reflected on the moment I made the commitment to ministry. I ran from it for a long time, but the moment I made the commitment was at my dad's funeral.

From an early age, my dad told me his wish for me to speak at his funeral. He reminded me many times over the years during random moments. My dad's desire for me to speak at his funeral was his passing the baton to me. Even though I never talked to my dad about my calling from God, he already knew. He prepared me. He knew and never said a word.

As I read those words from Dr. Wimberly's book, I wished for one more opportunity to talk with my dad. I wanted to know if he knew. But knowing him, he did. My dad would always say, "I got mine. You got yours to get." It took me years to figure out what exactly he meant, but reading Dr. Wimberly's book allowed me to understand that the baton had indeed been passed, and I was to continue the race.

A few weeks after I wrote the draft of this chapter, a mentor said to me out of the blue, "I remember your father's funeral. When you were speaking, he was in you. You have been on fire for the Lord ever since." My mentor's comment was confirmation that my dad's baton is still in my hand and I am continuing to run this race, but not in vain.

In moving with God's plan for my life, the ordination process included returning to school to obtain a Master of Divinity. After earning my doctorate degree in an eight-year uphill battle, I had no plans to ever return to the classroom as a student. But God's plan was different from mine.

As I progressed through this denominational requirement, I had many conversations with God. They went like this: "God, I can't. I can't go back to school. I do not have the money for tuition. I do not have the time to attend class. I do not have the energy to add another thing to my overflowing plate as a single mother of two active boys." In obedience to my denomination's process, I applied to a seminary that a mentor recommended. It was online, which would be less disruptive to my schedule. After the seminary president learned of my work responsibilities in higher education, he offered for me to conduct professional development for the faculty in lieu of half my tuition.

It seemed God was working out my seminary dilemma, until things started falling apart. Although I had been accepted to attend, I never received information on registering for classes, and my emails and calls went unanswered. In the meantime, I submitted a partial application to another seminary, coincidentally where my dad used to work. It was a partial application because I needed to submit another form and had not paid my application fee. A week later, I received a letter from the second seminary notifying me of my acceptance. *Wait, what, God?* I was thoroughly confused. How did I get accepted with a partial application? Was this a sign? Is that you, God? Was I supposed to attend the second seminary? I prayed and continued to weigh the pros and cons of each, but the decision-making was stressful. I was getting different advice from many people, and it all conflicted.

I was elated to put the seminary discussions on hold, as a much-anticipated Mediterranean cruise was just a week away. I was traveling with a large group and had been paying for this magnificent trip for 18 months. I even had a chat with God about my trip: "Dear God, I'm going on a fabulous cruise. Thank you for the financial provisions to pay for it. But, God, I do not want to deal with this seminary decision while I'm soaking up the sun. I will pray about it when I get back, okay?" How many times have you let God know when you would deal with something? I know it's not just me!

My mom and I headed to the airport, ready to board a plane to Rome and bask in the sun and sea for a week. My mind was clear of all things seminary-related. After meeting some of the travelers in our group, I noticed a distinguished, well-dressed man and his wife in our group. They were seated not far from us on the flight to Rome. When we arrived at the hotel in Rome, there was about an hour wait for our rooms. During one of my trips to the front desk to check on the status of our room, the distinguished gentleman and his wife were also speaking to the hotel representative. I asked the wife if her husband worked at or attended the second seminary because his lapel pin had the seminary's name on it. She said, "Baby, he's the president." I simply said to myself, *Okay God, I got it!*

During the cruise, I had several wonderful conversations with the seminary president, and he said he would look into financial help when we returned home. The day after he mentioned financial help, I received an email from his seminary offering a generous scholarship and confirmation that I could take my classes online. When I saw the president at our next meal, I asked if he had already spoken to someone about me. He said he had no plans to do anything work-related on the cruise—which meant God had worked out my seminary decision by providing a scholarship! I truly was free, with God's permission, to enjoy my cruise. Doesn't God always work out our problems! God works out our problems in God's own timing and in God's own way.

My reason for sharing all of this about my seminary decision is to emphasize two things—God's timeline and goodness. First, God's timing is not ours. God sets things up way in advance when we are either not thinking about it or still praying about it. I started paying for my Mediterranean cruise 18 months in advance. That means God already knew who was on the travel list for the cruise. God knew who was going to be on the cruise before I accepted my call to ministry. God knew well in advance that I would need to make a seminary decision and that the seminary president would be on the trip. Matthew 6:25-34 tells us not to worry. If God can take care of the birds, God will surely take care of us, even 18 months in advance. Let God work it out for you. Pray, trust and believe. God will show you the way before you even know where, how, and why you need to go.

Secondly, when God brings us to something, God will bring us through it. I told God all the reasons I could not attend seminary, and God removed each of my self-imposed obstacles. God tells us to believe and that the impossible will be made possible. *Through our weakness, he promises to put his glory and strength on display.* (2 Corinthians 12:9)

God may grow weary of our secular interventions because our plans often do not equal God's. Sometimes, God's plan is more significant. Scripture says, "The human mind may devise many plans, but it is the purpose of the LORD that will be established" (Proverbs 19:21). Even the Bible shares many accounts of the disrupted plans of women. It was not Hagar's plan to bear a child for Abram (Genesis 16:1-16), but she did and birthed a nation through her son, Ishmael. It was not Rahab's plan to hide two men in her home (Joshua 2:1-22), but she did and thereby exemplified her strong faith. It was not the widow's plan to give Elijah her last bit of olive oil (1 Kings 17:7-16), but she did and was obedient to God's promises. It was not Esther's plan to go before the king to save her people (Esther 4:1-17), but she did and was a beautiful vessel of God's grace for such a time as this.

To us, it makes sense to make plans, have to-do lists, and live by calendar entries. Particularly as women, we are taught to plan, including a plan B if plan A fails. As Former First Lady Eleanor Roosevelt once said, "It takes as much energy to wish as it does to plan," meaning a wish is not as substantial or sustainable as a plan. The point is, even in the midst of our detailed plan-making, when God moves, our plans get interrupted.

Plans made and even executed without God's permission get interrupted with God's plans for our lives. When God does interrupt them, our challenge is to listen and obey, knowing we can fully trust God. We have to listen and follow with 100 percent of ourselves, our faith, and our hearts. We cannot waver or worry, because such things are not of God. As difficult as it may seem, we have to trust God with our hearts and souls. We have to trust God, knowing that if God disrupts our plans, God is waiting to open the floodgates of heaven and pour out so much blessing that there will not be room enough to store it.

My life plan did not work out, but God's plan for my life has been better. God replaced my material losses with stability, God replaced my pain with joy, and God replaced my career with another one. I have learned to follow God with all my heart, soul, and being.

God's plan for our lives is God's own plan, not ours. When we choose to follow God, we exchange our dreams for God's plans for us with obedience, faith, and love. Let go and let God. Do not worry, God will light your path and make your ways straight.

CHAPTER 6: DEVOTION

The human mind may devise many plans, but it is the purpose of the LORD that will be established. (Proverbs 19:21)

QUESTIONS

1. Do you make plans without God's permission?
2. How has God interrupted your plans?
3. Are you open to hearing God's voice and making a change to your plans?

Prayer:

Dear God, we come before you with a spirit of gratitude; gratitude for disrupting our plans and redirecting our paths towards your glory. We are grateful for the bounty of your blessings; we are grateful for the renewed hope of a new journey; and we are grateful for the opportunity to pivot when

we make plans without your permission. Continue to feed us with your bounty, clothe us with your mercy, comfort and heal us when we are sick, hold us back when we are tempted, and uphold us by your omnipresent hands.* These and all other prayers we hold in the quietness of our hearts, we ask in your precious and mighty Son Jesus' name. Amen.

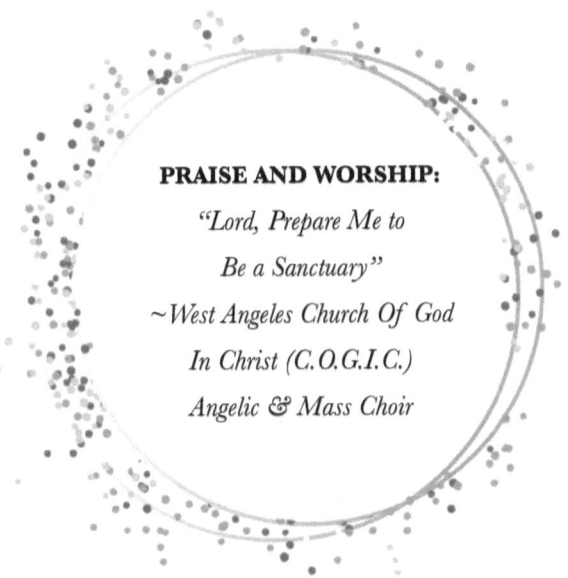

PRAISE AND WORSHIP:
"Lord, Prepare Me to
Be a Sanctuary"
~West Angeles Church Of God
In Christ (C.O.G.I.C.)
Angelic & Mass Choir

Chapter 7: S.W.E.

The following 15 guidelines to Redefining Life Through God's Grace were given to me by God as I transformed my journey from a holy mess to a message guided by the Holy Spirit. The journey was during a point in my life when I not only wanted to throw in the towel, but I had thrown the entire towel away. The guidelines are covered in God's favor. If you trust and pray, they will carry you through.

1. **Stop and Locate Your Breath; Stop and Locate Your Hurt**
2. **Let Go and Let God**
3. **Pray**
4. **Listen to You: You Know What You Need**
5. **Retreat**
6. **Reflect**
7. **Be Realistic**
8. **Be Open to Change**
9. **Do Not Be Afraid to Ask for Help**
10. **Do Not Be Embarrassed**

11. **Keep Your Circle Tight**
12. **Take Care of Yourself**
13. **Build Your Secondary Skill Set**
14. **Put One Foot in Front of the Other and Walk in Your New Destiny**
15. **Own the Game You Want to Win**

In a sermon I heard preached by African Methodist Episcopal Pastor Cynthia Parnell McDonald, Ph.D., she shared these powerful reminders: "Turn your obstacle into an opportunity. Turn your burden into a blessing. Turn your problem into a probability. Turn your junk into jewels. Turn your trash into triumphs. Turn your mess into a message. And, turn your pain into your purpose."[2] Dr. McDonald's reminders set my soul on fire, and I hope they will minister to you, too.

In the introduction to *S.H.E. Who Believed*, I shared the focus of this book through Luke 1:45: "And blessed is S.H.E. Who Believed that there would be a fulfillment of what was spoken to her by the Lord." The text begins with the blessing of "she". So, who is "she"? She is self-confident, highly favored, and equally yoked, even when faced with challenges. The *she* in this Bible verse refers to Mary, the mother of Jesus, but as you embark on this new journey and redefine your destiny, I want you to embrace S.H.E.—**S**elf-Confident Through God's Promises, **H**ighly Favored, and **E**qually Yoked.

SELF-CONFIDENT THROUGH GOD'S PROMISES

The fruit of that righteousness will be peace; its effect will be quietness and confidence forever. (Isaiah 32:17 NIV)

Mary was probably an early teenager preparing for womanhood and marriage when she received a visit from the angel Gabriel. (See Luke 1:26-38.) When Gabriel told Mary that she was pregnant with the Savior, she boldly said, "Here am I, the servant of the Lord…let it be with me according to your word." Mary was confident because she relied on the promises of God.

When God calls you to redirect your life, like God called upon the virgin Mary, you must be willing to serve and submit just as Mary in verse 38, "I am the Lord's servant; may your word to me be fulfilled." When God calls you to do something, you will have a period of processing and growth. Mary wasn't told the information in one moment, and then birthed Jesus in the next. There was a period of waiting and growth, both biological and spiritual. When you are faced with the task of redefining your life with God's grace, the same will be true of you.

After you find peace in being willing to follow God's plan, you have to let God use you. God used Mary as a vessel to birth the only begotten Son. What is God using you for? Wherever you are spiritually, you are already wrapped in God's embrace. Let God use you to accomplish your God-given task.

God calls each of us to a specific task, including you and me. When God calls us, like Mary, we must be willing to serve confidently. When plan A does not work out, you can confidently walk into your plan B using the steps in Chapter 5. Psalm 139:13-

14 reminds us that we were fearfully and wonderfully made in our mother's womb: "For it was you who formed my inward parts; you knit me together in my mother's womb. I praise you, for I am fearfully and wonderfully made. Wonderful are your works; that I know very well." Be encouraged in knowing that God created you to be a wonderful and confident woman, made in God's own image.

HIGHLY FAVORED

The angel said to her, "Do not be afraid, Mary, for you have found favor with God. (Luke 1:30)

Present day "Mary" is a good woman of the church. She minds her business and tries to live right. Maybe she is a Sunday School teacher, on the usher board, or sings in the choir. Maybe she is a stewardess of the church or just sits silently in the pews and prays for others. Whatever the case, Mary is going about her usual life. One day, an angel comes to Mary and says, "Greetings, you who are highly favored! The Lord is with you." Mary is a little taken aback. The angel continues, "The Holy Spirit will come on you, and the power of the Most High will overshadow you" (Luke 1:28; 35 NIV).

Whether Gabriel is telling the virgin Mary that she will conceive and give birth to a son called Jesus who will reign over Jacob's descendants forever, or whether Gabriel is telling the present day "Mary" that she is being called to make a life change, God has already worked it out. For no word from God will ever fail.

Whatever God has called you to do as you redefine your life,

God has already worked it out. Whatever God has instructed you to do, whatever task God has set before you, God has already worked it out. This is a lesson that we can take from looking at Mary. Everything worked out. Her situation may not have been perfect, but God worked it out. Joseph was scared and didn't know what to do. What would the people say about his fiancé being pregnant before the wedding? God worked it out. The Roman emperor, Caesar Augustus, issued a mandate that a census would be taken of the entire Roman world. This meant that Joseph and the pregnant virgin Mary had to travel from Nazareth to Bethlehem, since this was the town that Joseph's family originated from. God worked out their safe journey. When it was time for the virgin Mary to give birth, there was no room in the inn or any other place of comfort and convenience, but God worked it out and provided a manger in a stable for His son, the Prince of Peace, the Lily in the Valley, the Bright and Morning Star. Whatever God has in front of you, plan B has already been worked out.

EQUALLY YOKED

Do not be yoked together with unbelievers. For what do righteousness and wickedness have in common? Or what fellowship can light have with darkness?
(2 Corinthians 6:14 NIV)

Although theologians try to guess, they do not know much about Mary's childhood and upbringing. But there was something about Mary that God had already developed within her to make her the right one for the awe-inspiring task of carrying the baby Jesus.

Can you imagine what it was? How was she prepared mentally, emotionally, and physically to carry the Savior Jesus Christ? What was so special about Mary? Was it her lineage? Was it her connection to strong women in her family? Her peaceful spirit? Her racial background? We may never know, but what we do know is that she was equally yoked to do the work of God.

When you accept Christ as your personal Savior, you should not do all the things you used to do and go all the places you used to go. That is part of the equally-yoked process.

I would add that all opportunities in your life need to be aligned with your beliefs—your mate, your friends, your career, and your lifestyle. I shared that I wanted to be a principal, but the school system was toxic. I worked in the school system for 12 years, but a time came when the job and I were no longer aligned or yoked. God removed me from the situation and placed me in an equally-aligned atmosphere. When we walk with God, our Creator and Sustainer will light our path with a clear brightness.

Through *S.H.E. Who Believed*, I have shared my journey through divorce, into a new career, and then my calling into ministry. What are my next steps? I do not know, but what I am assured of is that God will guide and provide. Thus says the Lord GOD to these bones: I will cause breath to enter you, and you shall live. (Ezekiel 37:5)

I would love to remarry and share my life with the right person. I would love to bring women to God and help them through their storms. I do not know when or how, but God knows. That is all I need because this self-confident woman is covered by God's favor and is being prepared in God's yoke. And this I know, because I am S.H.E. — *S.H.E. Who Believed.*

QUESTIONS:

1. Have you ever believed in and for something, but God was not ready for you to receive your blessing?

2. Did you handle the wait with patience or impatience?

3. What are you believing God for in your current circumstance?

4. Do you believe God ordained your belief? How do you know?

Most Gracious and Omnipotent God,

I believe in your promises and your divine Word. Help me to remember to listen for your voice and assurance when I make plans, because they will not happen until you fulfill them. Help me to wait patiently for your blessings or your gentle (or not-so-gentle) nudge in another direction. You will direct my paths with favor and grace. In your Son's name, Amen.

PRAISE AND WORSHIP:
"Tis So Sweet to Trust in Jesus."

S.h.e.

**Self-Confident Through
God's Promises,
Highly Favored,
Equally Yoked.**

Devotionals

REDEFINE YOUR LIFE WITH GOD'S GRACE

I.

Stop and Locate Your Breath.
Stop and Locate Your Hurt.

The Lord will fight for you, and you have only to keep still. (Exodus 14:14)

Some nights, I have difficulty sleeping. I am up from 2am-4am, just wide awake. Often, it's because recent occurrences that bothered my spirit are running through my mind and I can't let them go. What lesson does God want me to learn from these experiences? Were my expectations too high of others? Was it me?

My mind usually wanders to the movie *The Color Purple* and the song "God is Trying to Tell You Something". As Shug Avery was leaving Harpo's Juke Joint on her way to the church pastored by her estranged father, she sang these words, "Can't sleep at night; And you wonder why; Maybe God is tryin' to tell you something." In other words, it is important to listen for the Word of God during the midnight hour.

When God speaks to us, whether it is in the middle of the night or as we go about our regular day, there is a message in God's word. Do you stop and listen, or continue to press on? When God speaks, we have to pause and receive the message. Often, the message is to provide us with direction, encouragement, and discernment. Especially during the times when you're hurting, allow yourself space and time to pause. Exodus 14:14 tells us, "The Lord will fight for you, and you have only to keep still." The pause is for God to prepare you for battle so that God can fight them for you. When God is trying to tell you something, take heed, sis.

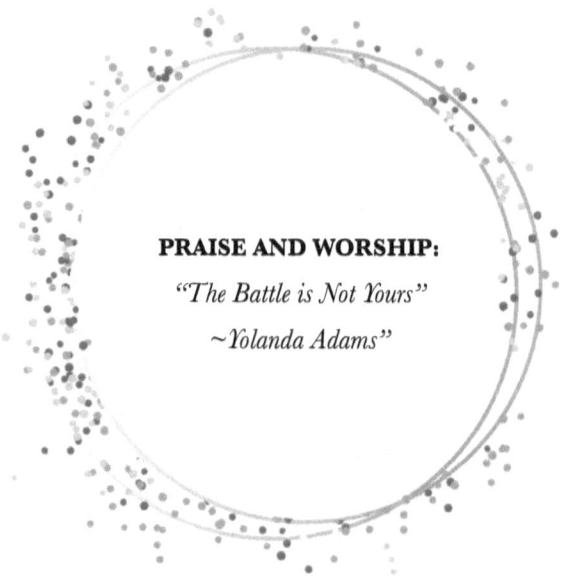

PRAISE AND WORSHIP:

"The Battle is Not Yours"
~Yolanda Adams"

QUESTIONS

1. Do you think God has been trying to tell you something?
2. If you have not been listening to God's Word, why not?
3. If you listened to God's Word, what happened?

2.

Let Go and Let God

Cast your burden on the Lord, and he will sustain you; he will never permit the
righteous to be moved. (Psalm 55:22)

I always need to know the next step, the next move, the next
event. For the past four years, I have taken groups of my college
students to Cuba. One summer, instead of going to metropolitan
Havana, we visited the mountainside of Santiago de Cuba. The
tour guide took us to the Sierra Maestra Mountains to retrace the
steps of Fidel Castro, Che Guevara, and others during the Cuban
Revolution. At the end of this two-hour hike, we visited Fidel's
mountain hideout. I asked a million questions because I could not
see a path in the direction the guide was pointing. Not to mention,
we were climbing an island mountain in June. It must have been 300
degrees. I really wanted to know when and where we were stopping.

I was surprised that there was no clear path to follow. I was
expecting this to be like an American tour, with carefully paved and
manicured paths with signs and guard rails. But on this tour, no such
luxuries were present. No pavement, no path, no guard rail, and no
signs. "Why isn't this path paved if these tours have been available
for decades?" I asked. We were going through rugged terrain, and
most of us were not wearing appropriate shoes or clothes. We did
a lot of grunting and sweating our way through lifting the weight

of our entire bodies to climb high steps and rocks, pushing each other up, holding each other so no one would tumble, guiding each other by grabbing each other's hands, pulling each other out of mud holes—trusting that we'd find the way in the absence of signs. The colorful language along the way was real. My students were in tears. They fell and scraped their legs. We were all frustrated. It was one of the hardest physical experiences of my life.

My A-type personality students and I learned that we had to give up our need for control and Americanized expectations to make it through the mountain. When we released our control, I took notice of my students. At first, they said things like, "Mind over matter," "Be like Nemo: just keep swimming," and "We can do this" or "We got this." They even made references to the college's hymn phrase, "Undaunted by the fight." But as the mountain got steeper, as the rocks got higher, and the mud got more slippery, and the tears of frustration began to fall for all of us, a student got out her iPhone and played Kirk Franklin's "Do You Want A Revolution?", turning up the volume to its maximum level. She then transitioned to some soul stirring hymns. Through falls, scrapes, bruises, breakdowns, and pushing each other to persevere beyond their perceived abilities, my students did not forget to call on God. Those first feel-good sayings only lasted for a few minutes, but when the going got tough, they knew to sing, pray, and praise God through that mountain of adversities. While we struggled to climb up and back down the mountain, the lessons in adversity were worth the temporary troubles.

When we give up control, God takes control. When we give up

control, God makes a way. When we give up control, God continues to supply our needs. Take that thing you're trying to control, release it, and give it to God.

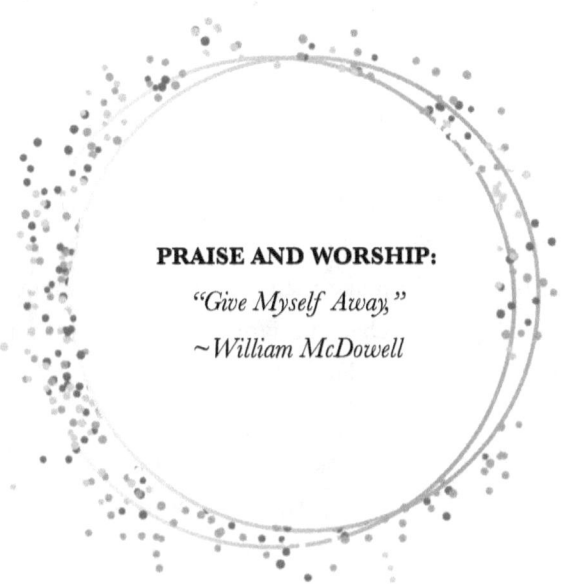

PRAISE AND WORSHIP:

"Give Myself Away,"

~William McDowell

QUESTIONS

1. What is it that you need to give to God?

2. What is stopping you from releasing it to God?

3. How can you find the strength to release it to God?

3.

Pray

Then you will call upon me and come and pray to me, and I will hear you.

(Jeremiah 29:12)

One of Aretha Franklin's well-known songs, "I Say A Little Prayer," was originally written for Dionne Warwick in 1966. Aretha and her Sweet Inspirations backup singers were warming up before a show, singing "I Say A Little Prayer," when it became clear to them that they should make their own version. Although Aretha's version never quite reached the fame of Warwick's version, it did reach number ten on the Hot 100 chart and number three on the R&B chart.

The song's secular lyrics, although written for a love interest deployed during the Vietnam War, reminds us when to pray. Aretha sings that she pray for her love the moment she wakes up; before she puts her make on; while combing her hair; when wondering what dress to wear; when running for the bus; when she rides the bus; and, all through her work day.

Through her lyrics, Aretha reminded us of the Apostle Paul's words from 1 Thessalonians 5:17, to "pray continually." We should pray to God at every step of our day. When we wake up, while we're doing the simple chores of the day, while we are at work, in the car, at home, in the store, at school, at church. All day, every day, we should pray to God.

This leads to the question, why should we pray continually? If God knows what we need, why should we pray? When we read the Bible, God speaks to us. When we pray, we have the opportunity to speak to God. We pray to thank God. We pray for the Holy Spirit to dwell in our heart and soul. We pray for direction and discernment. We pray for centering and peace. We pray for the wellbeing of our loved ones, neighbors, and the larger community.

Our prayers can be simple and from the heart. We're not competing with others to develop well-planned and articulate prayers. God hears our prayers, whether we are at the altar, kneeling beside our bed, in the car, or on the job. God takes our prayers with and without subject-verb agreement. God takes the five-second "Jesus, help!" to the five-minute prayers spoken by the church elders.

As you go about your day, say a little prayer. Say another little prayer this morning. Say a little prayer at noon. Say a little prayer in the car. Say a little prayer this evening. Say a little prayer for each other. Say a little prayer for your church. Say a little prayer for the sick and shut-ins, and those grieving. Say a little prayer for you.

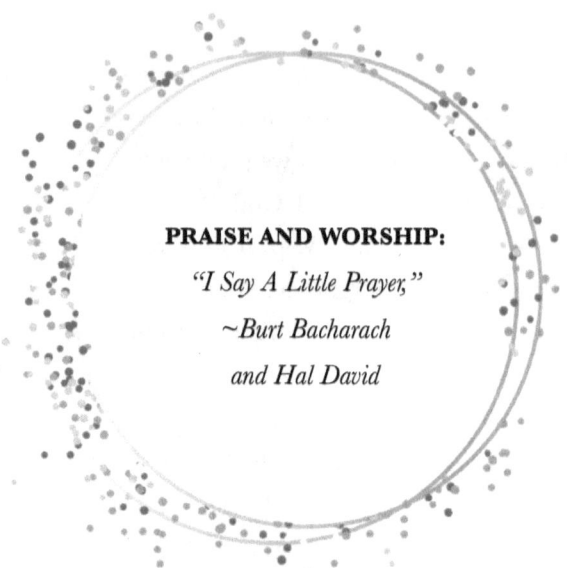

PRAISE AND WORSHIP:

"I Say A Little Prayer,"
~Burt Bacharach
and Hal David

QUESTIONS

1. Is it easy for you to pray?
2. Is it easy for you to pray for others?
3. How can you commit to a more fulfilling prayer life?

4.

Listen to You. You Know What You Need.

I will instruct you and teach you the way you should go; I will counsel you with my eye upon you. (Psalm 32:8)

The Bible tells us in Genesis 1:1-2 (NIV), "In the beginning God created the heavens and the earth. Now the earth was formless and empty, darkness was over the surface of the deep, and the Spirit of God was hovering over the waters."

Just as the Holy Spirit knew which way to hover over the waters as the heavens and earth were being created, the Holy Spirit still knows, even today, which way to hover in your situation.

When we live by the Holy Spirit's discernment, God tells us the right way to go. When we listen for God's voice, God's nudge, God's touch, God's gentle feeling—that is the Holy Spirit guiding our way. This is the same Holy Spirit who hovered over the oceans to create this awesome earth, and who continues to guide our steps today.

The Holy Spirit shows us the way when we have an open heart and mind. When we are open to God's Word and will for our lives, the Holy Spirit directs our path and makes our way straight.

The next time you need to know the way, lean not on your own understanding. Listen for God's voice. The Holy Spirit will center you, guide you, protect you, and lead you along the right way to go. Continue to walk with God, and God will continually walk with you. Amen.

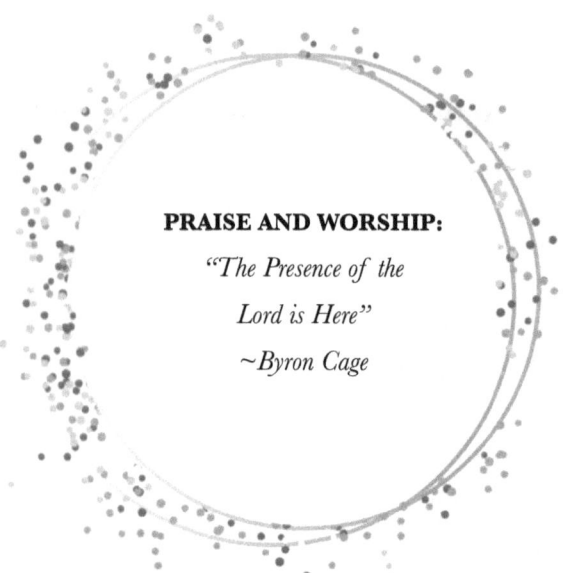

PRAISE AND WORSHIP:

*"The Presence of the
Lord is Here"*

~Byron Cage

QUESTIONS

1. Reflect on a time when the Holy Spirit guided you. What happened when you allowed the Spirit to guide you?

2. What does it feel like when you experience the Holy Spirit?

5.

Retreat

And when he had sent the multitudes away, he went up into a mountain apart to pray: and when the evening was come, he was there alone. (Matthew 14:23)

I tried to complete an overdue task, but I could not focus. I could not get it together. I was totally overwhelmed with life. The feeling would not go away. Finding the mental capacity to complete our tasks with excellence is clouded by the challenges of life. We have too many things to do and not enough time to do them— spouses, children, extended family, work, church, caregiving, health, finances, home repairs, and the list never seems to end. Whatever the dilemma, we are all overwhelmed with something.

In our seasons of feeling overwhelmed, we must make time for two things: God and rest. God should be the most important priority in our lives, but the order of our daily grinds doesn't always reflect God's first place position in our lives. In addition to finding more time for God through Bible study, prayer, and sharing God's love with others, let us also remember to rest in God's peace and love.

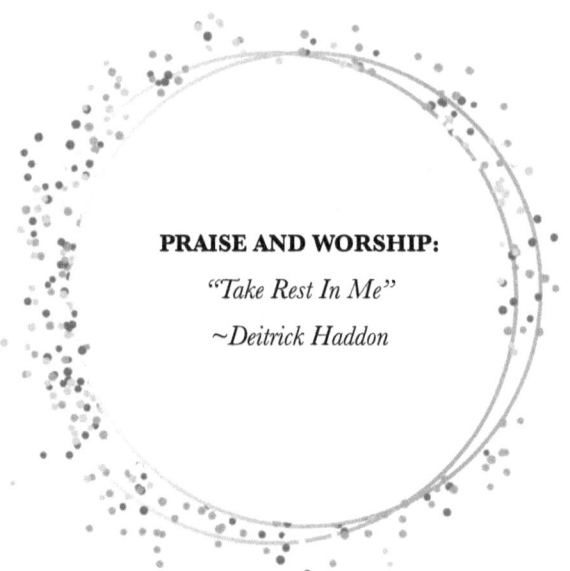

PRAISE AND WORSHIP:

"Take Rest In Me"

~Deitrick Haddon

QUESTIONS

1. What can you do to focus more on God?

2. What needs to be removed or added to your life for this to happen?

9.

Reflect

So if anyone is in Christ, there is a new creation: everything old has passed away; see, everything has become new! (2 Corinthians 5:17 NRSV)

When we reflect on our lives and the next steps God is calling us to take, sometimes we do not know what God is calling us to do. The scripture tells us that the old has passed away and the new has come. Is it okay that we do not always know the next steps? Of course it is!

When Jesus was overwhelmed with life and ministry, He went to the mountains alone to pray. Jesus prayed and reflected. He prayed and waited for a word from His Heavenly Father. I often think of the daunting task Jesus's disciples had in telling Him in Matthew 14 that his cousin, John the Baptist, had been killed. At first, Jesus retreats to a secluded place to be alone to process this information. But, the people were in need. Five thousand of them, plus women and children, were gathered and needed food, but the disciples only had five loaves of bread and two fish. Jesus looked toward heaven, prayed a blessing, divided the elements, and had them distributed so that everyone was fed—plus leftovers!

After Jesus met the needs of the people, He continued His retreat in a boat across the lake. Although He traveled with the disciples across the lake, He eventually went into the mountains alone to pray.

Even in His grief, Jesus helped His people. He met their needs before He took care of His own. In this account of His activities, Jesus gave us a blueprint. He retreated after God told Him what to do, then He went to God to get His next steps. That is what we must do. Retreat to God alone for an answer.

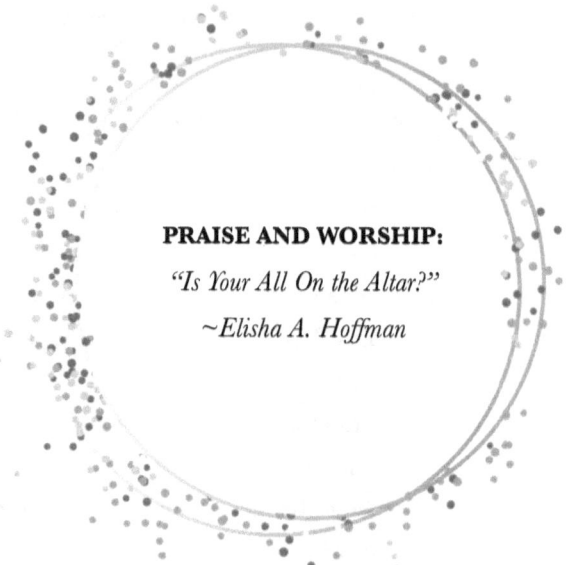

PRAISE AND WORSHIP:

"Is Your All On the Altar?"

~Elisha A. Hoffman

QUESTIONS

1. Do you know what God is calling you to do next?

2. If yes, how do you know?

3. If no, how can you create a space or place of retreat to hear God's Word?

4. When you hear the Word of God giving you your next steps, will you be open to doing it?

7.

Be Realistic

Do not be conformed to this world, but be transformed by the renewal of your mind, that by testing you may discern what is the will of God, what is good and acceptable and perfect. (Romans 12:2)

After my divorce, I had to learn to live with less money. I was drowning with my mortgage, daycare fees, monthly car payment, credit card debt, and the rest of my expenses. I tried getting a modification through my mortgage, but it was still too expensive. I put my house up for sale and cried each time someone came to view it. I was heartbroken to leave my beautiful home and supportive neighbors. I loved my community, but I could no longer afford to keep up with the Jones's when I was only operating with a little "j" compared to their all capital "J-O-N-E and S." I returned my car to the bank and moved into a townhouse. My mom financed a car for me and paid the monthly payments. My parents paid many of my monthly bills, and my aunts and uncles helped, too. My village surrounded me with financial help and love during this time, but I had to learn to live with less. Less money, less house, fewer luxuries, fewer vacations, and fewer things in general. Was it easy? Absolutely not. But it was my new reality that I had to accept.

Part of letting go is realizing you may have to face a consequence. For me, I had to let go of two houses: the one I lived in and the one I rented. I drove my car to the bank and left the keys in the night deposit box. In doing these things, I released my financial burdens, but the consequence was that my credit score took a significant nosedive. I had to be prepared for that. No, I was not happy downsizing and driving a car I didn't like, but I had to be realistic with my current space and place in life. I was in transition and operating under a temporary setback. This was not easy.

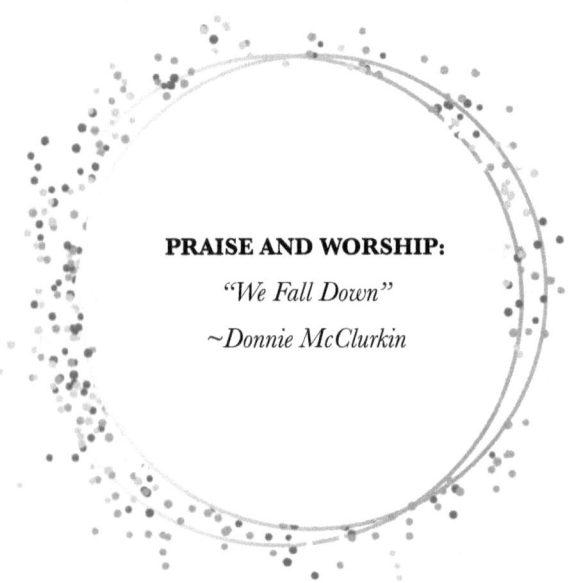

PRAISE AND WORSHIP:

"We Fall Down"

~Donnie McClurkin

QUESTIONS

1. Are you holding onto something that is weighing you down financially, emotionally, spiritually, or mentally?

2. If yes, why can't you let it go?

3. What do you need to move forward?

4. What is the consequence of not letting it go?

5. Create a plan to help let it go. It's time to move on, sis.

8.

Be Open to Change

Put away from you all bitterness and wrath and anger and wrangling and slander, together with all malice, and be kind to one another, tenderhearted, forgiving one another, as God in Christ has forgiven you. (Ephesians 4:31-32)

Many of us love Psalm 23. It is soothing to our soul and gives us the peace of God. I once saw Psalm 23 with a simple change that made all the world to me as a woman. It read and sounded differently because the scriptures spoke directly to me. Add your first name in place of the blank line and then see if you notice the subtle, yet powerful change starting at verse 1:

The Lord is _____ shepherd, she shall not want. He makes _____ lie down in green pastures. He leads _____ beside still waters. He restores her soul. He leads _____ in right paths for his name's sake. Even though _____ walks through the darkest valley, she fears no evil, for you are with her; your rod and your staff— they comfort _____. You prepare a table

before her in the presence of her enemies; you anoint her head with oil; _____ cup overflows. Surely goodness and mercy shall follow _____ all the days of her life, and _____ shall dwell in the house of the Lord her whole life long.

When we personalize the Word of God, it becomes a personal word to us. When you read your Bible, make it a point to add yourself to the scripture. Allow God to speak to you. Allow God to use you. Be open to receiving God's word as you open yourself to both change and the next steps in your life.

PRAISE AND WORSHIP:

"Changed"

~Walker Hawkins

QUESTIONS

1. When you read the personalized version of Psalm 23, did you feel closer to God?

2. How can you incorporate more time with God that is personally meaningful to and for you?

3. What is your favorite scripture?

4. How can you personalize it?

7.

Do Not Be Afraid to Ask for Help

God is within her, she will not fall; God will help her at break of day.
(Psalm 46:5 NIV)

Have you ever had one of those days when nothing seemed to go as planned? The kind of day that makes you want to crawl back into bed? The kind of day that makes you feel like you're walking backwards instead of forward? I'm sure you can relate.

There's a well-known children's book titled, *Alexander and the Terrible, Horrible, No Good, Very Bad Day*. It tells the story of how Alexander's day goes from bad to worse. When I have one of these days, I call it "An Alexander Day."

One Alexander day started off with a confusing dream. I woke up around two o'clock in the morning, wrestling with its meaning. The rest of my day seemed to be the same. As I was lamenting to God about my terrible, horrible, no good, very bad day, I thought of my boys who had been fighting in the morning. Their brotherly love was being expressed in a negative way, which was causing us to run late, and God reminded me that I had prayed for children even after the doctor said I couldn't have any. My boys were my blessing from God. Someone is praying for a child and wishing to be a referee every morning.

Then I reflected on my talkative and energetic class. They never seemed to calm down, but God reminded me to be grateful for a job and to be grateful for students who enjoy my teaching. After all, I did tell them at the beginning of the semester that I did not like a quiet classroom. Their banter was a direct reflection of my goal for the class. They were a community of learners who engaged in the intellectual process. Then I thought about the class I had to miss due to a parent-teacher conference I had to attend at my son's school. Maybe missing that class was one of my students' needed break or moment to decompress.

Then there was the highway traffic on the way home and the car that cut me off and wouldn't let me over, so I missed my exit and had to drive 12 minutes out of my way. When I finally got off, the traffic was so heavy that I sat on the exit ramp through five light changes— there was just nowhere for me to go. The blessing is that I was in my car, on my way to my heated home, ready for dinner. That's a blessing to reflect on because at one point, I lost my home and car and didn't have the money to heat my house or buy groceries.

As we reflect on these terrible, horrible, no good, very bad days, there's still always room to find a moment for praise and gratitude. While my day may have been off, someone else in the world had an even worse day. Even when all hope seems lost, God reminds us of our daily blessings. For every sad moment, God gives us a blessing. Whether small or large, we have to focus on God's daily works in our lives and how we can turn pain into joy.

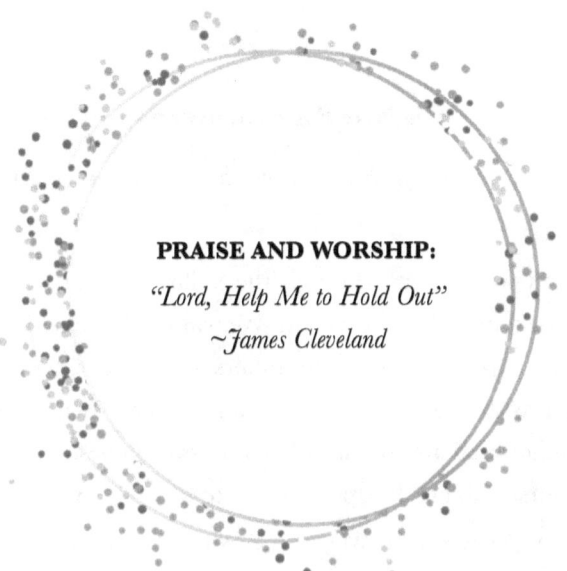

PRAISE AND WORSHIP:

"Lord, Help Me to Hold Out"

~James Cleveland

QUESTIONS

1. When you are having an "Alexander Day," how can you ask for help?

2. If you have a hard time asking for help, what will make the ask easier?

10.

Do Not Be Embarrassed

Cast all your anxiety on him, because he cares for you. (1 Peter 5:7)

When we're going through the valley, sometimes we feel the need to be a model superwoman. We want to be there for everyone, especially if we have children or others who depend on us. We brush our pain aside and push past the agony. This is not healthy and causes emotional and physical harm to our bodies. It is okay if you allow yourself to cry. It is permissible to let it all go and cry.

When Jesus visited Mary and Martha's home, He saw their profound sadness at the death of their brother, Lazarus. Seeing their tears, along with everyone else's in the house, Jesus began to weep. In John 11:35, Jesus wept. He cried because He felt their pain. If Jesus could cry in moments of sadness, we can, too.

Give yourself grace and space when you're going through the storm or a bad day. God will comfort you, sustain you, and brighten your days. God will bring a joy like no other. Press on and keep praying, my sister. A breakthrough is coming.

PRAISE AND WORSHIP:

"Give Thanks With
A Grateful Heart,"
~Don Moen

QUESTIONS

1. Why do you think women feel that they must carry the load without pausing to cry or taking time for themselves?

2. Can you think of instances in your life when you held in the pain without releasing it?

3. Who can you call on when you need a good cry?

II.

Keep Your Circle Tight

Perfume and incense bring joy to the heart, and the pleasantness of a friend springs from their heartfelt advice. (Proverbs 27:9 NIV)

Read Psalms 139:1-16, which says:

> *O LORD, you have searched me and known me.*
> *You know when I sit down and when I rise up;*
> *you discern my thoughts from far away.*
> *You search out my path and my lying down,*
> *and are acquainted with all my ways.*
> *Even before a word is on my tongue,*
> *O LORD, you know it completely.*
> *You hem me in, behind and before,*
> *and lay your hand upon me.*
> *Such knowledge is too wonderful for me;*
> *it is so high that I cannot attain it.*
> *Where can I go from your spirit?*
> *Or where can I flee from your presence?*
> *If I ascend to heaven, you are there;*
> *if I make my bed in Sheol, you are there.*
> *If I take the wings of the morning*
> *and settle at the farthest limits of the sea,*

even there your hand shall lead me, and your right hand shall hold me fast.

If I say, "Surely the darkness shall cover me, and the light around me become night,"

even the darkness is not dark to you; the night is as bright as the day,

for darkness is as light to you.

For it was you who formed my inward parts; you knit me together in my mother's womb.

I praise you, for I am fearfully and wonderfully made. Wonderful are your works;

that I know very well.

My frame was not hidden from you, when I was being made in secret, intricately woven in the depths of the earth.

Your eyes beheld my unformed substance. In your book were written all the days that were formed for me, when none of them as yet existed.

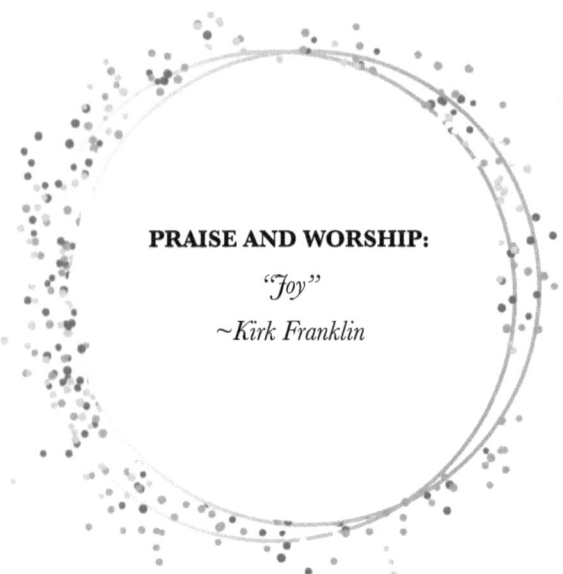

PRAISE AND WORSHIP:

"Joy"

~Kirk Franklin

QUESTIONS

1. After reading Psalm 139, list three words that come to mind. How did it make you feel?

2. You were fearfully and wonderfully made by God. What does that mean to you?

3. Verse 16 says, "Your eyes beheld my unformed substance. In your book were written all the days that were formed for me, when none of them as yet existed." This means that even when you were still in your mother's womb, God knew what you would be doing today. God knew your journey before it began, which means God already has a solution. How can you dwell on God today and find peace in your future journey?

12.

Take Care of Yourself

Do you not know that you are God's temple and that God's Spirit dwells in you? (1 Corinthians 3:16)

Jeremiah 1:4-10 says:

> The word of the LORD came to me, saying, "Before I formed you in the womb I knew you, before you were born I set you apart; I appointed you as a prophet to the nations." "Alas, Sovereign LORD," I said, "I do not know how to speak; I am too young." But the LORD said to me, "Do not say, 'I am too young.' You must go to everyone I send you to and say whatever I command you. Do not be afraid of them, for I am with you and will rescue you," declares the LORD. Then the LORD reached out his hand and touched my mouth and said to me, "I have put my words in your mouth. See, today I appoint you over nations and kingdoms to uproot and tear down, to destroy and overthrow, to build and to plant."

Much excitement and pride surrounded the movie, "Black Panther." It's filled with rich themes and meaning, unbelievable action, and futuristic technology.

For me, the most powerful moment came in a quiet and solemn

conversation between T'Challa and his deceased father, T'Chaka, as they spoke in the ancestral plane after T'Challa won the challenge and went through the royal rituals to become king of Wakanda. T'Challa quickly admits to his father that he is not ready to assume the throne. He is not ready to assume the position of power as his father had before him. He was not ready to be king without his father's earthly presence. T'Chaka lovingly responds, "A man who has not prepared his children for his death has failed as a father."

As I cried through this scene, tears streamed down my face and my youngest son asked why I was crying. I was crying for two reasons. First, I miss my dad. Life without him has been a difficult journey. I was imagining having that same opportunity as T'Challa, to see and speak with my deceased dad. That had to be a wonderful and uplifting experience.

My second reason for crying was the thought of both my earthly father and God preparing me to go forth and do great things. Just as God tells Jeremiah, "Before I formed you in the womb I knew you, before you were born I set you apart," when we were in our mothers' wombs, God prepared us for a time such as this. God prepared us for our current situations. God prepared us for success. God prepared us for failure. God prepared us for increase. God prepared us for decrease. God prepared us for health and vitality. God prepared us for sickness and frailty. God prepared us for life.

How awesome it is to know that we are prepared for this very moment in time. God has predestined us. God tells us what to do and puts the words in our mouths. Just as T'Challa received confirmation of his upcoming journey, the Bible shows us the way. God's words provide confirmation for our destiny. And just like T'Challa, we have to listen, obey, and trust our Heavenly Father. God tells us to not be afraid. God tells us that everything is or will be worked out.

Since God has it worked out and has predestined you for your journey, walk in God's favor and go forth. Go forth and do God's will. Not just today, but every day. Let others see God inside of you.

As you reflect on "Black Panther" and this scripture today, think about how God has spoken to you to show you your future. You were prepared for it. Are you ready to walk *in* and *to* it? God has prepared you for your future. Let God lead the way and walk in your destiny. God has already mapped it out and done it for you. Wakanda forever. God forever.

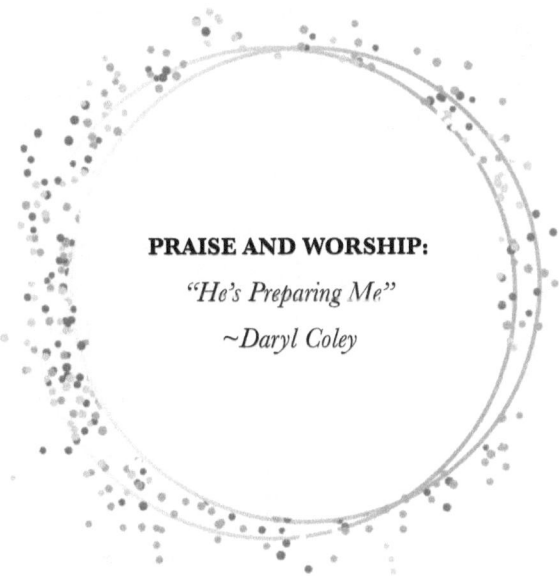

PRAISE AND WORSHIP:

"He's Preparing Me"

~Daryl Coley

QUESTIONS

1. Are you ready to walk in the destiny that God has planned for you?

2. If you are not ready, what is stopping you?

3. If you are ready, what are you waiting for?

13.

Build Your Secondary Skill Set

For this very reason, you must make every effort to support your faith with goodness, and goodness with knowledge. (2 Peter 1:5)

In 2005, I was on pregnancy-related bed rest, 24 hours a day. Needless to say, my sleep schedule was completely disrupted. I spent the majority of my time watching the news, movies, and documentaries. In August, a category five hurricane was forecast for the Gulf Coast region. The impending Hurricane Katrina became the focus of every news channel as the storm proceeded towards landfall. It was expected to be catastrophic, potentially causing great destruction to the area. I watched day and night and became consumed by the people's experiences before, during, and after the hurricane. It was heartbreaking to see the devastation caused by the levees breaking in New Orleans: the loss of lives, the stranded residents in the Superdome, the lack of government response, and the media's contrasting coverage of people's experiences in different parts of the city based on race and class.

My keen interest in Hurricane Katrina led me through the years to continue to follow the recovery process, read books, and watch follow-up media coverage. When the ten-year anniversary of the event was approaching, I created a college course for students to study themes of education, psychology, history, political science, economics, sociology, environmental science, religion, the arts, and health in the recovery process.

In my course preparation and securing speakers for class discussions, I am amazed at the resiliency, faith, and positivity of the people who endured so much loss and heartache. I reflect on a few of our course speakers — a former co-worker, former principal, and a former medical resident, each of whom experienced Hurricane Katrina differently, but each with the same fortitude.

My former co-worker rode out the storm with members of her family in the Superdome. The sights, smells, and feelings that she recounted were ones that journalists could not adequately portray. The former principal detailed her process of preparing the first floor of her school for the hurricane. She and the custodian moved books, important documents, and other items to higher levels in hopes of their safe-keeping during the storm. The former medical resident shared the process of manually pumping life into patients who could no longer breathe without electric-powered ventilators after the storm's fury. She stayed at the hospital for days until the last patients were moved to safer locations.

Their stories not only inspired us all, but are a testimony of God's strength and love during and after the storms in our life. No matter what we endure, God is in the midst of troubling times. My former co-worker became my co-worker after she had to relocate from New Orleans to find a home and employment in a new city. The former principal's school was destroyed in the storm and all the school district employees lost their jobs following the hurricane.

The former resident had to finish her medical preparation in a new city. They all pivoted, rebuilt, and found goodness in their faith and knowledge of God's promises.

PRAISE AND WORSHIP:

"Yes You Can"

~Marvin Sapp

QUESTIONS

1. How have you found goodness in the midst of your storm?

2. How can you share your testimony with others?

14.

Put One Foot in Front of the Other and Walk in Your New Destiny

All our steps are ordered by the LORD; how then can we understand our own ways. (Proverbs 20:24)

"You have brains in your head. You have feet in your shoes. You can steer yourself in any direction you choose. You're on your own. And you know what you know. And YOU are the one who'll decide where to go..." This quote comes from the book, *Oh the Places You Will Go* by Theodor Giesel, better known as Dr. Seuss. This book is often given to graduates, as it shares tidbits for your life ahead. But sis, I ask you, can you really steer yourself in any direction you choose? Are you really on your own? Most importantly, will you know what to do?

So, we know what Dr. Suess says, but what does God say? One of my favorite Bible scriptures, Isaiah 30:21, states, "Whether you turn to the right or to the left, your ears will hear a voice behind you, saying, 'This is the way; walk in it.'"

God will show you the way. You do not have to find it yourself. But you do have to listen to God's voice. You cannot be caught up in the world. Be caught up in God's Word. God promises to show you the way. You just have to listen.

I'm sure you've had times in your life when you've had to listen to and heed God's Word. Sometimes it's not an easy or popular choice. Sometimes God takes you against the grain, but God will always show you the way.

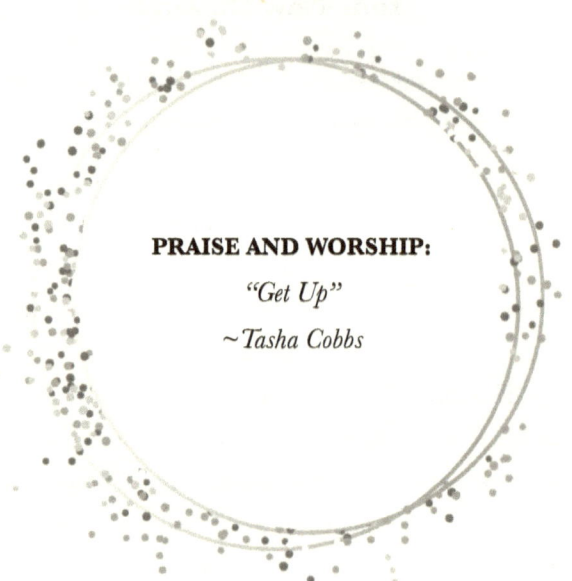

PRAISE AND WORSHIP:

"Get Up"

~Tasha Cobbs

QUESTIONS

1. Reflect on a time you did not allow God to guide your way. What happened?

2. Reflect on a time you allowed God to guide your way. What happened?

3. What was the difference between these two occasions?

15.

Own the Game You Want to Win

No one after lighting a lamp puts it under the bushel basket, but on the lampstand, and it gives light to all in the house. (Matthew 5:15)

Slay
Just do it
Be lit
Be poppin'
Get your glow on
Go big or stay home
Kill it

Through the years, I know you have heard, "A first impression is a lasting impression." No matter what you're doing, you never know who's watching. Be amazing. Be on fire for God. Let your light shine. God wants you to be lit.

"You are the light of the world. A town built on a hill cannot be hidden. Neither do people light a lamp and put it under a bowl. Instead they put it on its stand, and it gives light to everyone in the house. In the same way, let your light shine before others, that they may see your good deeds and glorify your Father in heaven" (Matthew 5:14-16).

Use your God-given light to see your way through. Use your God-given light to shine above the rest, and never let anyone dull your shine. Do not be afraid to be the most prepared. Do not be afraid to rise to the top. Do not be afraid to increase your walk with God.

Though I have been teaching for 25 years and often receive cards and expressions of gratitude from my students, my greatest compliment came at the end of a semester. A few students shared in front of class how much they enjoyed the course and my teaching style. One student said she appreciated me because she could see the God in me through my teaching. Be so lit for God that God manifests in your professional life just as much as in your personal life. I don't mean that you have to quote scripture all day. What I mean is that others should see the God in you through your daily walk and in your talk. It's a sense of humility, a sense of peace, and a sense of stability.

PRAISE AND WORSHIP:

"This Little Light of Mine"

QUESTIONS

1. Has there been a time when you decreased your flame to let someone else shine?

2. Why did you let their light shine?

3. How can you shine your light for God?

For as in one body we have many members, and not all the members have the same function, so we, who are many, are one body in Christ, and individually we are members one of another. We have gifts that differ according to the grace given to us: prophecy, in proportion to faith; ministry, in ministering; the teacher, in teaching; the exhorter, in exhortation; the giver, in generosity; the leader, in diligence; the compassionate, in cheerfulness.
(Romans 12:4-8)

Closing Prayer

. . . .

Most Gracious and Eternal God,

I thank you for grace—your love, given freely
even when I am not grateful. I thank you for
the lessons in the valley that took me to the
mountain top. I thank you for provision and
your gifts that are unique to me. Help me to
use my gifts to glorify you in all ways,
on all days. Allow me to walk
to my purpose as only you can.
May your glowing light surround me, may
your never-ending love enfold me, may your
perfect power protect me, and may your
omniscient presence watch over me always.
In Jesus' name.
Amen.

Notes

....

- *Adapted from Jarena Lee, *Religious Experience and Journal of Mrs. Jarena Lee, Giving an Account of Her Call to Preach the Gospel.* (Published for the author, 1849).

1. Edward P. Wimberly, *Recalling our own stories: Spiritual renewal for religious caregivers.* (Minneapolis, MN: Fortress Press, 2019), 1.

2. Cynthia Parnell-McDonald, "Power of Faith." (sermon, North Atlanta District Conference, Christ Community A.M.E. Church, Clarkston, GA, January 4, 2020).

About The Author

. . . .

REV. ANDREA DAIS LEWIS, Ph.D. is an ordained servant of God who delivers God's word with a sweet spirit and in the authenticity of her ancestors. After experiencing a season of loss and detours, Dr. Andrea empowers women to successfully navigate the pivots of life. She is an Associate Minister at Big Bethel African Methodist Episcopal Church in Atlanta and founder of Virtuous Pearl Interdenominational Women's Ministry, which studies God's word through the experiences of women.

Dr. Andrea values and models academic excellence. A summa cum laude graduate of Spelman College, Dr. Andrea earned a Master of Science in Education from the University of Pennsylvania, Master of Divinity from Turner Theological Seminary at the Interdenominational Theological Center, and a Doctor of Philosophy from Georgia State University.

Dr. Andrea's past professional experiences include elementary school teacher, public and private school administrator, and college department chair. Through her current efforts as Director of Student Success and Associate Professor of Education at Spelman College, Dr. Andrea works to ensure students receive equitable resources.

Dr. Andrea authored four books, *Preservice Teachers, Social Class, and Race in Urban Schools: Experiences and Strategies for Teacher Preparation; Valerie's New Friends; Unsung Legacies of Educators and Events in African American Education*, (co-authored); and *S.H.E. Who Believed: Redefining Life through God's Grace.*

Dr. Andrea is a life member of Alpha Kappa Alpha Sorority, Incorporated and member of Jack and Jill of America, Incorporated; The Links, Incorporated; National Alumnae Association of Spelman College; and, YMCA of Metro Atlanta Board of Directors.

Her proudest accomplishment is being a mother to two amazing sons.

FOLLOW DR. ANDREA D. LEWIS

- Official Website: https://www.drandrealewis.com
- Facebook.com/drandrealewis
- Instagram: drandrealewis
- Twitter: drandrealewis